20 CEDAR ST

A TRUE STORY

To MY Friend,

Michael Anthony Yoke.

Hope You enJoY the Story.

20 CEDAR ST

First Edition Published July 2016

Identifiers:

Library of Congress Control Number: 2016910521

Softcover: ISBN-10: 0-692-71988-1

Softcover: ISBN-13: 978-0-692-71988-6

eBook: ISBN-10: 0-692-75219-6
e-Book: ISBN-13: 978-0-692-75219-7

20CedarSt@Gmail.Com

20 CEDAR ST

A TRUE STORY

JASON SALVINO

TABLE OF CONTENTS

Disclosure 5
Introduction 6
Chapter 1 15
Chapter 2 21
Chapter 3 32
Chapter 4 44
Chapter 5 52
Chapter 6 62
Chapter 7 70
Chapter 8 85
Chapter 9 101
Chapter 10 108
Chapter 11 121
Chapter 12 130
Chapter 13 146
Chapter 14 163
Chapter 15 175
Chapter 16 185
About the Author 196

DISCLOSURE

My name is Jason Salvino, and I will tell a true story of my recollections and memories of childhood at my family's 20 Cedar St home, and how it continued to influence me throughout my life. This story made me who I am today, but sometimes I wish I didn't have a story to tell at all. I wish I could've grown up like most other kids, normal.

There is so much more to tell about my own life, to include criminal-like behavior, but due to the negative impact it would have, I didn't have the desire to include it.

The profanity which occurred throughout the stories of my life has been edited, making the content of this book appropriate for readers of nearly all age groups.

Names, dates, and locations may have been changed or not added to this true story to protect the rights of others.

Introduction

My family's 20 Cedar St home is where the story begins. My great-grandfather migrated from Italy to America quite some time ago. It's hard to know exactly when he arrived, because nobody in my family ever cared to talk about anything. General knowledge and stories about life were never discussed inside the walls of 20 Cedar St, to include simple conversation.

My great-grandfather was told to me as being a hot tempered, average height, very stocky man, with light hair and colored eyes. He managed to meet the daughter of a wealthy family and quickly married. Somehow, my great-grandfather got his in-law's to pass down their family's 20 Cedar St home to him as time went by. The home was hand built by my great-grandfather's in-law's, and was even the home to where generations of their family was born. One of the in-laws born in that home never let it out of his site. No matter what time of the day, you could always look outside the window of 20 Cedar St and see him parked in front of the house. He would sit in his car for hours, staring at the home he was born in. He was the nicest man and loved 20 Cedar St more than anyone. I'm sure that deep down inside he was disgusted about losing his family's home, as he very well should've been. My family wasn't supposed to live in that home, it was built and filled with another family's memories. It was told by ancestors that 20 Cedar St was cursed for as long as we stayed in the home. The curse of 20 Cedar St was real and casted upon our family, to haunt every generation who lived inside.

During the Great Depression, my great-grandfather had to support his two newly born children, Susana and Fresco. Never being told much about the past, all I know is that my great-grandfather bootlegged alcohol on a fairly large scale during prohibition to support his family. He was a connected Italian man who enjoyed the rush of being crooked, and it was in his blood to do so. One of the very few things ever told to me about him, was that he was a mean bastard. Maybe that's the reason why his wife was buried with her own parents when she passed away and not with him. A few years after his wife passed away, my great-grandfather fell down the back stairs of the 20 Cedar St home. He split his head open on a large radiator heater at the bottom, killing him near instantly. The cursed home had taken the life of the first 20 Cedar St family member.

As time went by, my grandfather and his sister Susana grew into young adults. My aunt Susana married and took the last name of her husband and moved out of the 20 Cedar St home. She had two children of her own, but the curse never forgot her, striking down upon her with obesity and finishing her off with cancer. My grandfather had assumed ownership, and was the sole recipient of the cursed 20 Cedar St home for many years to come.

The name "Fresco" isn't my grandfather's true name, he simply acquired that nickname from his sister when he was just a child. That nickname stuck with him for the rest of his life, with few people ever knowing or addressing him by his real name. My grandfather also had the criminal mind like his father. He actually began to build his gambling enterprise when he was just a teenager. While serving in WWII, he ran crap tables at the military camps and made a good profit. He had a warmer side to him than his father though, and would give half of his winnings to the homeless Germans. My grandfather eventually met his future wife, and they went on to marry after his return from serving in Germany during WWII.

My grandfather was average height, had colored eyes, light hair, and was a very handsome man. He was the slickest of talkers and knew how to speak to people. He was able to slide his way in and out of anything. He was known to many as a gambling entrepreneur and was an extremely connected Italian man, enough said! He not only knew, but was very close to all kinds of people, including movie celebrities, mob bosses, and even the heavyweight champion of the world. He was friends with Rocky Marciano, who would often come to the 20 Cedar St home to meet with my grandfather. I asked my grandfather if the Rock

8

was a big guy and he said, "His shoulders were so wide that he had to turn sideways when he walked through the kitchen doorway." My grandmother told me that she once served Marciano a large T-bone steak, but became upset at him on that occasion. She told me that after the Rock finished his meal and whatever business he had to take care of with my grandfather, he didn't thank her for the food.

My grandparents wanted children and were so excited when their two kids were born, my uncle Vincent and my mother Giuliana. I often reminisce and look at the few old photos I was able to salvage over the years and see the love in my grandparent's eyes, and just how truly happy and proud they were of their children. My mother and uncle Vincent grew up with everything they wanted, with a good chance of becoming successful, and the possibility of conquering the 20 Cedar St curse which they never knew existed. My grandfather sent them both to catholic school where they academically excelled. My uncle was becoming an extremely talented musician and my mother a scholar, as both of my grandparent's children were on their way to success.

Some years went by, my mother and uncle had graduated high school and were in their early twenties. They had begun to party just like most young adults would do. My mother was a good looking woman, had dark hair, brown eyes, and had just met a red headed stunner named Douglas.

My uncle Vincent stood six feet tall, had colored eyes, light hair, and was very broad shouldered. He managed to meet a blonde haired sweetheart named Sarah. My mother and her boyfriend, as well as my uncle and his girlfriend had begun experimenting with drugs, which would eventually spiral out of control. Pills and heroin became the choice of drugs for the 20 Cedar St children and their partners in crime. Before they knew it, both of my grandparent's children were addicted to heroin and any pills they could get their hands on. Their partners became drug addicts just as fast.

As more time went by, my mother became pregnant by Douglas and Sarah became pregnant by my uncle, with both drug addict woman continuing their pill and heroin use all the way to the delivery room. My uncle Vincent would soon enough marry his girlfriend Sarah, who gave birth to my only first cousin and heroin addicted newborn, Vincent Jr. Months later, my mother gave birth to her own heroin addicted newborn, my older half-brother, Tony.

Douglas had become the son in-law to a connected Italian man and was proud of it. He loved his son and the mother of his child, but loved something else much more. Just six months after my brother's birth, my grandparents were vacationing with my mother and little Tony about one-hundred miles away from 20 Cedar St. Douglas had decided that he wanted to stay back home and wasn't interested in going on the trip. It was only a few days into the vacation when my grandfather received a phone call from the 20 Cedar St police department, explaining to him and my mother that Douglas was found dead at home. The curse ended the life of the first man to become part of the 20 Cedar St family, and it was no surprise that he couldn't even get past the first year. My grandfather ended the vacation early and everyone returned home.

Even with the death of her husband, my mother continued to take off for days at a time, stealing and shooting up drugs. She would continuously leave little Tony to be taken care of by his loving grandparents. My uncle Vincent and Aunt Sarah had already moved out of the 20 Cedar St home some time earlier, and were living in an apartment down the street. They enjoyed shooting and swallowing drugs as a lifestyle, which took over their lives and begun to destroy another cursed 20 Cedar St life. My cousin Vincent Jr didn't have a chance.

After Douglas' death, my mother quickly moved on and found a very nice Italian man named Emilio Salvino, who wasn't a United States citizen at the time. He had dark hair, dark eyes, and was at the beginning stages of drug use. He came from a very large and decent family who had migrated from Italy some years earlier. Emilio was a hard worker and enjoyed a fairly honest living, but over time that would change. After Emilio married my mother and spent time inside the cursed 20 Cedar St home, he began using pills and heroin at an alarming rate. Before you knew it, my mother was pregnant with my older sister, another child born with drugs in her system and already addicted to heroin. My mother continued using heroin, and just one year later gave birth to her third heroin addicted child, myself, "Jason Salvino." Just one year later, my mother was pregnant again with her fourth child.

My father had been pushing drugs around town and was occasionally getting arrested for minor criminal acts from what I've been told. Eventually, he got locked up for dealing heroin and was on the verge of getting deported from the country because he never became a permanent citizen. I was told that he got permission from the courts to appear at the hospital to see the birth of my little sister before being deported. My little sister was the only one of us born without heroin pumping through our veins, and it wasn't because my mother had become a changed woman. The reason for a clean birth was simply because my mother was serving a prison sentence of her own, and the correctional facility did their best to ensure she stayed clean while pregnant and incarcerated. Every 20 Cedar St child was born without a leg to stand on, and most of us with heavy drugs already flowing through our veins.

I was only two years old when the judge had granted the visit for my father to see my younger sister's birth, and I never saw or heard from him again, ever. He later found employment in Italy, remarried, and even had a few more children. Just when he thought he was safe, the 20 Cedar St curse caught up with him. The previous years of shooting up drugs had left my father with a gift that kept on giving.

With everything that was going on, and my mother's eyes constantly rolling into the back of her head, my grandfather refused to accept that his daughter was a drug addict by her own hands. He believed that others were a bad influence, and she would never use drugs on her own.

My grandfather was running underground casinos up and down the coast. He made a wealthy living hustling others, and was able to support our entire family. He would hold private casino nights and host games such as Craps, Poker, and Barboot. He worked alongside the very best mechanic in the business, as they would use electromagnet crap tables with powdered magnetic dice. There was a hidden switch inside of a sliding wooden panel underneath the table, which allowed it to be operated by a remote control. My grandfather and his partners were able to control the magnetic dice, allowing the players to win or lose at the houses discretion. With my grandfather always gone and my mother always out getting high, I would really have to praise my grandmother for trying to raise and take care of us.

My grandfather never allowed my father's family to come around or visit any of us, even after his deportation. He blamed my father Emilio for getting my mother involved in drugs, just like he also blamed dead Douglas. My grandfather always blamed others and would never believe his own children were drug addicts on their own. He would never believe that they were the ones stealing from people and department stores, in order to purchase more drugs to feed their addictions. The very large Salvino family was forced to stay away for life, and I never knew that they even existed. I especially didn't know that they lived just minutes away from 20 Cedar St all the years I lived there.

Chapter 1

I can only remember my childhood back so far. My earliest recollection of any memory is somewhere around the time when I was nearly six years old, when my grandparents packed the four of us and our mother into their Chevrolet Caprice. My grandfather had the unforgettable, *grandparents are special people* license plate on the front of his car. Louis Prima was playing in the cassette player like always, and we headed to our vacation cottage on the coast. We would go there on occasion during summer break and have plenty of fun at the beach. We ate like kings, and would barbeque and boil lobsters in the backyard of the cottage. I remember going to ride the go-karts, smashing them to hell with my brother Tony. We crashed the go-karts until we were kicked off the track, forcing my grandfather to use his muscle to quiet the attendants down. My cousin Vincent Jr was only able to make it on vacation when his parents weren't in a heroin induced coma.

One day that week in the backyard of the cottage, my mother was preparing to barbeque on the grill, but put a bit too much lighter fluid on the charcoal. My mother was strung out on drugs and holding my little sister in her arms when she lit the oversaturated coals. The coals had burst into flames, burning my mother's forearm pretty fierce, forcing our family to the hospital immediately. Needless to say, we ended that vacation early and headed back to 20 Cedar St.

Almost immediately after the barbeque burn to my mother's forearm, she had gone back to normal, staying out and about with drugs in her system. There was definitely something unusual about her being gone that time though. Normally, she would come home from time to time in an effort to clean up and ask my grandfather for money. I was told that my sister who was not even a full year older than me, used to change my diapers when nobody was around. I hadn't seen my mother in over a week, and before I knew it, I was looking at her closed casket at the local funeral home. I was nearly six years old, and being so young I didn't know what to think. My family never talked about anything, so nobody had yet discussed what happened to her.

Soon after my mother's funeral, my grandmother finally decided to tell us what had happened. She explained to us that our mother died from complications due to the burn on her arm from the barbeque blaze. We all believed the story and that is what we were always told. My grandmother also felt the need at that time to tell us the story of how my brother's dad had died years earlier at 20 Cedar St. She told us that he had been struck in the head with a baseball bat by some local punks while at a convenience store, and later died at 20 Cedar St of a hemorrhaging brain aneurism of some sort. Those were the stories that were told to us, the stories that we all believed, and the stories that nobody dared to question. If we dared to even ask about the details of either one of their deaths, my grandmother would become irate and end the discussion quickly. I wasn't able to ask questions about my father either, or any part of the Salvino family, leaving that side of the family a complete mystery to me.

I was growing up fairly normal, considering that I didn't have any parents. I was living a life that didn't allow questions and had no answers, so I just stopped asking and forgot about what I wasn't supposed to know.

As a child, I remember going down to the local cemetery very often with my grandmother to put flowers on my mother's grave. She would always comment on how nice the headstone and entire gravesite looked, and would place new flowers at the base of the stone weekly. It was the largest stone in the cemetery and was shaped as a large Jesus Christ nailed to the cross. People would always stop by and place flowers as if it was a shrine. I was around the cemetery so often, which was just down the street from 20 Cedar St, that I eventually started to dream about it. I used to have three distinct dreams, over and over for years to come following my mother's death.

The first dream would consist of all my family visiting my mother's gravestone. We would all

17

stare at the stone and my grandmother would talk to her deceased daughter. After the visit was over, everyone would walk away, but I would stay for some reason that I could never understand. My mother's burnt arm would come out from underground and pull me under with her. I would be so scared in the dream that I was unable to scream or ask my family for help. I would wake up very scared in the middle of the night, but even as a kid I would ask myself, "What is my mother trying to tell me?"

The Second dream was of myself hearing my mother call me for help, deep from within an empty water well or deep hole in the ground. I could hear that she was in some sort of struggle, so I would jump into the deep hole and free fall all the way down, until inches before I could see what was going on, or what was happening to her. Every time I would have this dream, I would wake up just before I was able to see my mother, never to reveal what was happening to her or who was doing it.

The third and final dream was of myself visiting my mother's gravestone, but it was at a different cemetery. I would be sitting at my mother's footstone simply talking to her, then a man would approach from behind and shoot me in the back. My mother would then drag me underground with her.

I always had so much on my mind, but I couldn't say anything because nobody at 20 Cedar St wanted to talk about it. Everyone just wanted to forget about my mother's death and move on as if nothing had ever happened. I could only wonder what my brother, sisters, and Vincent Jr were going through, and how they were feeling. As we all got older I took a look back, and couldn't remember a single time that any of my siblings and I had ever once talked about our personal problems together.

Being a bunch of messed up kids, I guess my grandparents thought that sending us all too catholic school when we were younger would help. My grandmother was a true believer in the catholic religion, so she sent us all to catechism classes after school as well. I remember catechism very clearly, as the classroom was filled with kids, to include my best friend. I remember the very religious cate-chism teacher asking me a direct question in the basement of the church where classes were held. He said, "Jason, why do you believe in god?" I answered him, "I don't." I could see the smoke begin to come out of his ears like a volcano. He then said in a loud voice, "*What do you mean, you don't?*" I then told the catechism teacher, "There is no such thing as god, because if there were, all the horrible stuff that goes on at 20 Cedar St wouldn't happen." He then gave me some bull-crap religious answer, so I told him what I thought about god. I said, "There's no such thing as god, just maybe the devil!" The volcano erupted with great force, and the catechism teacher got in my face and screamed in the loudest possible voice, "*You A-Hole, get the hell out of this church!*" I truly thought he was going to strike me, but with mutual understanding between the two of us, that was my last day of any official catechism classes.

My grandmother was very adamant about me becoming a catholic and was later able to convince me to complete my remaining catechism classes with a new teacher. My best friend's mother began teaching the catechism classes to her son and myself at the kitchen table of her home. She loved me like her own son, and would bake fresh brownies every night that I would attend. She never liked to see me struggle in life, and knowing how I already felt about religion, she would read the catholic scriptures out loud to me. Once she saw that I just couldn't listen anymore, she would complete my workbook questions for me and release us outside to play.

I eventually completed the catechism classes, fought through my first communion, and engaged in battle with my confirmation. I was finally finished with the torture that my grandmother so desperately wanted me to endure, but I am proud that I was able to make her happy.

Chapter 2

Growing up in a very special family, or dysfunctional as I heard others call it, would eventually become normal to me. Over time, my brain adapted to the way of life at 20 Cedar St, and I couldn't tell the difference between normal and dysfunctional anymore.

The only structure that we had at 20 Cedar St was the clockwork of my grandfather's fellow hustling partners, who would show up every Sunday morning at five o'clock to go over business. I would get up early and go downstairs to the first floor kitchen and would try to listen to what they were talking about. I would put my ear to the wooden door, but could never hear anything but mumbles, they even whispered in their own house. My grandfather would always know when I was at the door and he would open it about two inches to talk to me. He knew what I wanted and would let me run in really quick to get a doughnut. When I was grabbing my pick of doughnut, I would try to take a look on the table to see what they were doing and he would say, "Now get out of here, hurry up." This was probably the only organized, structured, and supervised activity that ever went on at 20 Cedar St, everything else was an unorganized mess. My siblings and I used to play unsupervised all day long around the neighborhood, and I'm very surprised that none of us were ever abducted.

I remember when I was about seven years old and was going nuts trying so swat at a bee in the backyard. My brother Tony and younger sister soon jumped in to help, but couldn't swat the bee either. I decided to run into the garage to find something to kill the bee with, but the only tool was a spading fork hanging on the wall. I quickly ran out of the garage to find the bee, but discovered that it was already swatted down and under the crushing blow of my younger sister's foot. With absolutely no supervision, added to the lifestyle we had at home, it seemed ok for me to drive the spading fork through my sister's foot in an effort to kill the bee a second time. Luckily, because of my inaccurate strike, only one of the forks hit her foot, but went clean through, leaving a half inch wide puncture going in through the top and nearly coming out from the bottom. I then received a large butt whooping from my older brother Tony.

I couldn't blame myself for using the spading fork, it was the only tool that we owned, other than a Phillip's head screwdriver and a butter knife which was used to replace a flat head screwdriver that broke years earlier. My grandfather kept his two-piece mighty tool collection in a shoe box in his bedroom closet. The spading fork was truly the only thing in the garage and the only yard tool we owned, so I grabbed it. My family was not very mechanically inclined, being in the unique business that my grandfather was in. He had guys that did everything around the house for us, so I guess he had no need for tools. I always wondered why in the hell we kept a spading fork hanging in our garage anyway, never mind it was our only yard tool.

As a kid, I had a severe problem with torturing and killing whatever animal, reptile, or insect I could get my hands on. This must've been my own source of therapy, since there was nobody at home willing to talk to me about the problems that went on at 20 Cedar St. I would go down to the local pond which was inside the cemetery from the time I was about seven years old until I was almost twelve, for hours at a time. I would enjoy catching bullfrogs with a hook and a small red piece of cloth attached to it, and of course my favorite, catching snapping turtles.

After catching each bullfrog, I would walk about sixty yards to the access road which led to the freeway and would wait for the eighteen wheelers to come driving along. I enjoyed throwing the bullfrogs in front of the trucks in an effort to time it just right, so they would explode when hit by the fifty mile an hour front grill. I enjoyed every kill so much that I would run back to the pond anxious to catch more bullfrogs and would repeat this for hours. I can remember my favorite childhood torture pastime very well though, it was when I would catch a snapping turtle, and those moments were equivalent to Christmas morning for me. I needed

23

extra privacy for those torturous events, so I would take the large turtle's home to my backyard and acted out twisted crucifixions, but enjoyed them very much. Using a fairly large rock and some very long nails that I had found over time, I would drive the nails through the turtle's feet, very deep into the ground, just like I saw Jesus on my mother's grave-stone that I visited so much. Once the feet were nailed in place, I would pour some of my stashed gasoline in a perfect circle around the turtle, just like I saw on television from devil worshiping mov-ies. I would then saturate the entire turtle in gaso-line and light only the outer ring on fire. The turtle would begin to panic from having the fire and scorching heat around him. The turtle would rip his arms free of the nails tearing his flesh, and would then try to escape by walking through the fire, only to send its entire body up in flames. That part was very exciting for me, and I would let the turtle run around in panic until the fire would go out. I would due this over and over until the snapping turtle had no feet or legs remaining to nail into the ground. I would then finish off the turtle with a blow into the soft side of the body using the famous spading fork from the garage wall. With nobody to look over me, these were the things I did to self-sooth. There was something special about that spading fork, and over time it would develop a special relationship with me.

When I was about eight years old, my uncle

Vincent started staying at our 20 Cedar St home with us more often. At six feet tall, and at that time over three-hundred pounds, he was beating up on my aunt Sarah and Cousin Vincent Jr pretty bad. My grandfather didn't want to see his only son and last remaining child go to jail, so he would send my aunt some money and agree to take my uncle back to the 20 Cedar St home until things smoothed out. Turning near permanent and for many years to come, my uncle would live with us at 20 Cedar St. He allowed me to have some of the most memorable pastimes possible for any child. Very lucky for us though, my uncle knew that if he touched us kids, my grandfather would kill him, or at least that's what I believed at first.

I can go back to one of my first memories of my uncle Vincent when I was about eight years old. He would bring me downstairs to the first floor of the 20 Cedar St home where his bedroom and living area was, and have me roll marijuana joints for him inside the top of a shoebox cover. He would normally be wearing no shirt, but at times he would have his favorite ripped up green dog racing T-shirt on. He would never have any pants on and was normally wearing just his white brief underwear with so many holes and rips, he might as well have just worn nothing at all. His balls and penis were scarcely covered and hanging freely in the air, staring me directly in the eyes while rolling his joints. The standoff between me and his genitals to include his butt and crack, was very similar to an old west gun duel. While I was rolling away, he would smoke pot and blow every hit into my face, trying to get me high and laughing in his creepy voice, "Ha, ha, ha." Once stoned, he would make his way to the piano for an hour long jam out session, then pass out.

My uncle Vincent had this incredibly distinct voice, which even today I cannot get out of my head. I don't know if it was the drugs he was on or not, but most of the time he would talk as if his jaw was wired shut. His lips would open but his teeth would remain closed and he would speak in this grinding, gritty, freaky as hell voice. That voice really did stay in my head forever, and for some reason I am able to mimic his voice to the exact.

My uncle seemed to always have scabs over his body, and of course being a kid I would ask him what they were. He told me that the scabs were spider bites, and that his bedroom was infested with bugs. As I got older, I realized that the spider bites were actually from his "Junkie itch", and just the overall use of heavy drugs. It was pretty gross at times and even scarier at night when he would occasionally tell me his twisted bedtime stories. I would have to bet that I am one of the few individuals in the world to have ever been told childhood bedtime stories to that caliber. I was still about eight years old or so and Uncle Vincent would come up to my room and tuck me in, just like normal kids would get tucked into bed. He would be extremely high as always and insist on telling me a bedtime story. My uncle told me that the story he was going to tell me was a true story. Years later I was able to prove some of the story true, but the fictitious sounding stuff could never be determined as fact or fiction, because nobody was there to determine otherwise.

Now imagine the six-foot-tall, three-hundred-pound man with scabs all over his body, talking with his gritty voice as if his mouth was wired shut. He would also be wearing no shirt and his torn briefs that were pretty much just the elastic band with a couple small patches of cotton. Here is my most memorable bedtime story out of the few of them.

"Once upon a time, there was a man named Paul Rasini, and he had a gay bastard son named Johnny. The two of them lived just down the street from 20 Cedar St. Paul was known around town as a tough guy, and was extremely disgusted that he had a gay bastard of a son. Whenever Paul wanted to toss the football with his son, Johnny would insist on playing with his Barbie dolls instead. This upset Paul and made him beat Gay Johnny all the time. He beat and tormented Gay Johnny so much, that he turned retarded and still very gay. I remember walking by their house one day when I was younger and Gay Johnny was outside playing with his dolls. He told me, 'Hey Vincent, I have to go drain my carrot.' I hated when he said drain my carrot, it made me want to kill him! I then told his father Paul that if he ever needed a sitter for Johnny, I could help out with that. I offered my services because I wanted some alone time with Johnny so I could torture him. I was finally able to house sit for Paul and watch over Gay Johnny. He was a teen-ager, but I still had to give him a bath because he was retarded. I would undress him and tell him to get in the water. While he was in the bath playing with his dolls I would get pissed off, so I decided to get a toaster and plugged it into the bathroom electrical outlet. I dropped the toaster in the bath water, and zapped the crap out of that gay bastard. Gay Johnny started to shake and he yelled, '*Noiye, noiye, noiye, noiye, noiye, noiye!*' I then unplugged the toaster and decided not to zap him anymore, but just thinking about when he would say, 'I have to drain my carrot,' made me decide to zap him again. '*Noiye, noiye, noiye, noiye, noiye, noiye,*' he yelled as electricity jolted through his gay body. I told him not to tell anyone about what happened or I would do it again. A few years and many beatings later by his father, Gay Johnny hit his father over the head with a hammer at their home just down the street. His father was knocked unconscious and Gay Johnny set the house on fire hoping that his gay hat-ing father would burn to death in it. I remember seeing the smoke that day coming from Paul's house and ran over there. The fire department had just arrived and they went inside the home and saved Paul. As they were putting out the fire, the police showed up and asked me if I knew who may have done it. I told them that it was Gay Johnny. Ever since that day, nobody has ever seen or heard from Gay Johnny again, but I will never forget, noiye, noiye, noiye, noiye, noiye, for as long as I live. Ha, ha, ha! The End."

That bedtime story would really scare and terrify the crap out of me, understanding that my electro-cuting psycho uncle was living just a flight of stairs away. After hearing the story about five or so times, I began to enjoy it. I became the one asking my uncle to tell me the story about electrocuting the gay bastard Johnny all the time.

Even after hearing stories like that and crucifying animals, I was still a pretty good kid though. I would never really get into any big time trouble in my early childhood. Soon enough though, Uncle Vincent began to show me good ways to be more like him.

Starting around the time I was about eight or nine years old, my uncle would drive me around town, visiting some of the local supermarkets and drug-stores. He would have me wear these large jackets which probably belonged to his son Vincent Jr. After putting on these big multi-pocketed jackets, he would give me the game plan and blueprint layout for each store we ripped off. My uncle would say, "Walk straight and then go to aisle seven, in the rear of aisle seven there's a lot of Almond Joy candy bars, steal them, they're my favorite." He would tell me to fill up my jacket with as many as I could, which was maybe twenty.

My uncle was caught stealing so many times around town that he stood out like a sore thumb, so he would use that to his advantage. With him making his way into the store about twenty seconds after me, all eyes in the store were on him, so grabbing the candy bars or whatever else the job asked for was a synch. He would say to me, "Don't get nervous or you will screw up the whole freaking thing, once you get the jacket full, put your head down and walk straight out, don't you freaking dare stop to talk or answer to anyone, just keep walking." With all the stealing I had done, my uncle never once gave me a little meat off the bone.

After not receiving anything from the heists, I became a little upset, even as a kid. I decided to steal on my own at this age in order to get a little something for myself. There were two problems though, I didn't have the decoy of my uncle and I was a young kid alone in a store, which looked suspicious already. Around the age of nine years old, I had been caught stealing on two separate occasions and was escorted home by the police. I stopped stealing on my own from convenience stores for a while and had to settle for asking my grandfather for a dollar bill every few days.

About a year later and around ten years old, I was

approached by one of the neighborhood teenagers. He was about three or four years older than I was and told me that he had some toys for me in his garage attic. I was desperate for some new toys, so I went over to check out what he had. He actually did, all kinds of cool toys and gadgets which had mesmerized me. He said, "You can have one item for every time I can dry hump you." I was nervous and really didn't know what dry humping was, so I allowed him. I wasn't afraid of him; I was just terrified of everything as a kid. I was always scared and nervous because of everything I had been through, but mainly because I never had anyone to talk to about my problems.

When he was done dry humping, he allowed me to take my toy and go home. This only happened on one other occasion and just a few weeks after the first incident. I was walking down the street when he saw me. He told me from across the street to go to his attic for another toy, and I said "No"! He crossed the street and slightly intimidated me to go with him. Being such a scared kid, I went. That was the day he tried turning me gay. I first got to pick out a toy, and while he was dry humping away, he got sweaty and took off his shirt. He eventually tried to take my pants off and wanted to start screwing me I think. I pushed him off and ran home so terrified, never to go back inside that garage ever again. I've never told a single person about this incident until right this second.

31

<u>Chapter 3</u>

Even though my family was extremely special, everyone and their mother came to visit us on holidays and birthdays. My grandmother was a holiday fanatic, and I really appreciate the fact that she instilled such memorable holiday tradition in our family.

One of my favorite relatives who always made it to the house for holiday meals and birthday cake was my grandfather's older sister, Aunt Susana. She was in the record books for being the center of attention. She wouldn't be caught dead without wearing her extremely tight purple yoga suit that was begging for a little breathing room. She would also be wearing the matching high heel pumps that were ready to explode off of her extremely large and swollen feet.

Aunt Susana visited often in her later years at our 20 Cedar St home. She could be heard cursing as her enormously overweight body took physically demanding steps up the main flight of stairs which led to the second floor kitchen. For my aunt, a basic flight of residential stairs was like climbing the Empire State building. Each step had its own curse, moan, and groan, which sounded similar to a large animal being slaughtered. She would sound off as she began her climb, *"Ohhhhhh my god, holy crap, these freaking stairs! God, why do you do this to me? Jesus Christ almighty, why did you put these stairs on this earth, why are you punishing me? Ohhhhhh!*" After about three steps and then possibly a one to two-minute break, she would continue her treacherous voyage to the fourth step and so on. We always knew when Aunt Susana was visiting.

After about ten minutes, she would finally make it up the entire flight. She relaxed at the kitchen table calling for all takers to rub her feet and clean the jam from between her sweaty toes, due to the marathon she believed she'd just completed. The going rate was about twenty-five cents to bring her suffering legs and feet back to life. Pedestrians must've wondered if we were running a slaughter house inside, due to the horrendous screams that were heard as my aunt completed what seemed to be for her, the "Bataan death march!" Breathing heavily, my aunt would sometimes pop her dentures out onto the table to enhance her breathing and to scare us. From what I've been told, she was the toughest son of a gun you could ever come across in her earlier years. Too bad that my fearless aunt didn't stick around more often to keep my uncle Vincent in line, since my grandfather was always on the hustle.

I remember the only disturbing part about having friends over the house for birthdays and gatherings. It was when my uncle Vincent would show up outside on summer days with his extra special,

"Heroin induced surprises!" At times, my uncle would make his way to the backyard water hose, and would be completely naked with just a soap on the rope around his neck. He always complained that the old claw foot tub inside the house was too small for his large body to fit in. In the summer months my uncle enjoyed taking nude showers in the backyard, and I am the lucky one who has to remember the site of his grotesque body being bathed. Placing his thumb on the tip of the hoses nozzle, he would then spread his butt cheeks and spray pressurized water into his butthole. The lathered scrubbing of his butt, balls, and crack in the presence of the neighborhood was just another normal for 20 Cedar St.

I remember an unfortunate moment around the time I was nine years old, when Uncle Vincent was rummaging through all of my grandmother's clothes. This was a normal thing for him to do, as he would try to put together a couple dollars for some smokes or come up with the final few dollars for a fix. I eventually realized that he was having really bad heroin withdrawals when he would begin to look through my grandmothers clothes for money. I always hoped he would find a few dollars to buy his drugs, so he would go back downstairs to his bedroom and pass out. If we were to get really lucky though, he would overdose and die. Everyone in the family knew where my grandmother ate, stored, slept, and even showered with her money, in her bra. It was the only place she could keep all of us from stealing every penny she had. Legit casinos began to open in the 20 Cedar St area around this time, and my grandfather's underground gambling enterprise was gone. My family was officially dead broke ever since the enactment of honest gambling. Without enough money to support my uncles drug addiction, it had become very difficult for my grandparents to control his violent behavior.

After all of my uncles searching through the house for a couple bucks, while wearing his torn up briefs and no shirt, he wasn't able to find a penny. He approached my grandmother and told her straight forward, "Give me two bucks for a pack of smokes." My grandmother said, "Vincent, I don't have any money until the first of the month when I get my check." Grinding his teeth, he loudly said, "*I know where it is, now give it to me*!" My grandmother told him to get away and go downstairs, but my uncle wasn't leaving without his two dollars. He charged at my grandmother, ripped open her shirt, and went for the hidden stash of money located in her bra. My grandmother tried to keep her arms in front of her chest area in a hugging fashion, so he couldn't remove the money from out of her bra. That was when my uncle became enraged and decided that he was going to get the money no matter what. I can still remember when he opened his mouth and attach his teeth to the meaty outer part of my grandmother's forearm. He let out a very loud "*RRRRRRRR*" sound like a dog as he bit down, popping the majority of his teeth into her flesh. I can still remember the blood coming down her arm and the slight blood on his teeth. My grandmother grabbed the money out of her bra with her opposite hand and threw it at him. I remember standing in the corner of the room behind the kitchen door not knowing what to do. Actually, the truth is; I was too scared to do anything. I was such a chicken, that I can still remember my knees shaking so violently that I couldn't even take a step.

My uncle Vincent was getting worse by the day. For whatever reasons my grandparents had, they wouldn't throw him in jail, or at least kick him out of the house.

Just a couple months later, my older cousin Hanna, the granddaughter to my fearless aunt Susana, was watching the four of us while my grandmother was out playing bingo. After a few hours of peace and quiet, my uncle Vincent woke up from his drug induced coma to realize his junkie pills were gone. Without him understanding that he swallowed all of them before he blacked out, he put the blame on everyone in the house.

We had all taken our baths and were in our pajamas when we could hear the screams starting from downstairs. He was enraged and shirtless, wearing only his famous white torn up briefs as he started up the stairs screaming, "*Give me my pills, who stole my pills, I need my pills!*" He started to

36

chase after us, because he truly believed that a bunch of children had stolen his narcotics. This charade soon turned into a violent game of hide and seek. All of us were running around the house, trying to avoid the violent hands of Uncle Vincent. I remember being on the second floor of 20 Cedar St and realized that I was trapped in the living room. I could hear his screams from nearby and became so scared, that I opened up the window and lifted the screen. At that moment I was more than ready to jump out, risking my life to escape if he would've got to me.

My brave older cousin Hanna, just as brave as her grandmother Susana, had come up with a plan. One by one, she scooped us up and got us together in a football like huddle. Once we were all together, we started to move away from my enraged uncle's voice. We all made a dash down the stairs, out the front door, and piled into her little blue Chevy Cavalier. Screeching the tires, we were out of there, safe and sound, but we still had to return home since we had school the next day. She drove us around for hours until she saw that my grandfather was home. It was late, somewhere around midnight and we had all fallen asleep in the car. My cousin Hanna got all of us into the house and in our beds. Still to this day, I am indebted to my cousin for that act of braveness and her care for us. My uncle must've received some money from my grandfather or found a hidden stash of pills and passed out again. That type of behavior went on for a long time.

My grandmother always tried to put out the best meals she could for being the Italian family that we were. Dinner at 20 Cedar St only consisted of the three major food groups, spaghetti, lasagna, and stuffed shells.

One afternoon around the same time as the fore-arm biting incident, my grandmother was making our dinner, when Uncle Vincent suddenly approached the kitchen. He wanted a couple bucks for some more smokes. My grandmother told him the truth and said, "Vincent, I don't have any more money." His cowardliness quickly got enraged and grabbed the boiling pot of water off the stove and threw it at her. I don't know what part of her body he was aiming for, but he hit her in the chest area. Luckily for everyone, my grandmother was wearing her apron that day and only suffered a few minor burns on her neck and chest area.

There were definitely times when I wished I would've robbed a convenience store in my childhood and stolen all the cigarettes, so I could've thrown my uncle a pack of smokes like a dog bone every time he got enraged. I almost felt like I wasn't stealing him enough candy bars and it was my fault for his flare-ups.

Even though my grandmother would never call the police on my uncle Vincent, she would call the police when I would go missing. I used to hide from my uncle when he was having his withdrawal rages on days that I would be home alone. I would hide under my bed, in the attic, or in my closet under a pile of clothes. I would hide for so long that I would eventually fall asleep and nobody would find me until many hours later. I used to like hiding under the bed, because I could put my ear to the wooden floor and listen to where my uncle's location in the house was. I could never understand why my grandparents allowed this to go on for such a long period of time, but later in life I got a really good idea why.

Despite the fact that 20 Cedar St was cursed, and I was living a life outside of the normal, there was one special day each week that made me feel like the luckiest kid alive. Saturday mornings as a child are still a great memory for me. I would wake up to the aroma of my grandmother's century old recipe of homemade pancakes. No matter what was going on at 20 Cedar St, my grandmothers Saturday morning pancakes made all my problems go away. The feeling I had on Saturday mornings must've been the feeling that other kids had the majority of the time at their own homes. There could've been grenades going off around me, but I was undisturbed in my pancake fantasy world. Vincent Jr never made it much for Saturday pancakes, he was at his apartment down the street with his mom, with no intentions of coming over to be around his evil father.

I always wondered how bad it must've been for my cousin Vincent Jr, when it was just himself, his mom, and his lunatic father at the apartment down the street. I used to see a lot of my cousin when his dad was living with him. He always wanted to get away from his dad so much that he would spend a lot of time at our 20 Cedar St home. I can still remember when his mom would drop him off at our house. I would run outside excited to see him, but I would notice that almost every time he would arrive at 20 Cedar St, tears were still in his eyes from whatever his father had done to him. The reality was that my uncle was a violent, abusive, evil person, who would kick the crap out of him and his mom. My aunt Sarah would call my grandfather and tell him that she was going to call the police unless he got my uncle out of the apartment. My grandfather never wanted to see his last remaining child go to jail, and that is the reason why my uncle continued to live at 20 Cedar St for so long.

After many childhood years of having to live with my uncle Vincent, my aunt finally forgave him and allowed him to move back to the apartment. He was finally out of 20 Cedar St and we were all very happy, but I began to worry so much for Vincent Jr.

Soon after, my uncle, aunt, and Vincent Jr moved out of their apartment, or maybe they got thrown out, I really don't know. They found a new apartment complex to live at, which was also very close to 20 Cedar St. My uncle was extremely nuts at that point in his life. During his transition into his new apartment, he stopped by our 20 Cedar St home and asked my grandparents for a couple bucks. My grandfather gave him a dollar and some change and said, "That's all I have Vincent." My uncle immediately went down the street to the local gas station to get some cigarettes. He went inside the small attendant's booth and asked for his famous pack of non-filtered Camels. The attendant placed the cigarettes on the counter and rung up the item on the register. The price with tax came out to somewhere around a dollar-ninety or so, but my uncle only had about a buck-sixty. The attendant asked for the money and then counted it. The attendant soon realized that my uncle was short some change and asked for the rest. My uncle said, "That's all I have." The attendant went for the smokes in an effort to remove them from my uncle's death grip. After a quick struggle over the pack of cigarettes, my uncle removed his blade from his pocket and stabbed the man in the arm. The attendant released his grip and called the police. My uncle drove back to 20 Cedar St to tell my grandfather what he'd done, and to take a couple drags of his new smokes.

Through my grandfather's legal connections, my uncle walked away with a few days in the can and probably probation of some sort. If my uncle Vincent would bite his mother for two dollars or stab a gas station attendant for a pack of smokes, what would he do for something of more value I always wondered?

My grandmother was a faithful Catholic and always believed that 20 Cedar St was indeed a cursed home. She would always yell, "*God, why did you curse this house, why!*" She believed in the curse so much, that right around these problematic times she called the local church and requested for the priest to come to 20 Cedar St and bless our home, inside and out. She wanted the priest to walk through every room and remove the curse which had been destroying the lives of the people inside for generations. When the priest arrived to our home, my grandmother became very excited and asked him to come inside for a cup of coffee. I wasn't home at the time this happened, but my grandmother told me that the priest refused to come inside of 20 Cedar St. She asked him why he wouldn't come inside the home and he said, "I can see horrible demons in all the windows of the house, demons that are too powerful for me." She told him that he was a priest and was supposed to help, but he told my grandmother that he was sorry and couldn't enter into 20 Cedar St.

My uncle Vincent was having trouble paying rent at the new apartment complex he was staying at. He probably wasn't selling enough drugs at the time. It's also possible that he was swallowing and shooting everything up for himself before he could sell it. He asked my grandfather for money, but he told my uncle that he was broke.

After my uncle returned to his apartment to try to work something out with the manager, he found the eviction notice on the front door. Uncle Vincent, Aunt Sarah, and Vincent Jr got their belongings and were lucky to get into a nice condominium days later with the help of my grandfather. My uncle was still enraged and not that easy to shake. He decided to go back to the apartment complex that kicked him out and had a few words with the manager. He got back into his large silver Chevy Caprice that my grandfather had passed down to him and drove away. My uncle returned a few minutes later and approached the apartment complex front lobby at about thirty miles per hour, smashing right through the god damn building. I didn't see my uncle for a few months after that, so I would have to say that he got into at least a quick jail bid.

It's odd behavior for an adult to drive their vehicle through a building, but thinking back, I did the same thing. I was only five years old and left unattended in a running vehicle outside of a drug store. I got into the front seat of my grandmothers Oldsmobile Cutlass and mimicked what I saw her do when she drove. Seconds later, I had blasted through the front of the building.

Chapter 4

It was Christmas time again, and my grandmother did such a wonderful job of making me feel like a normal kid. I will never forget how much effort she put into Christmas day for all of us to enjoy. She had me believing in Santa until I was pretty old, but I guess she had me believing in a lot of things that weren't true. My grandmother made sure that Christmas was magical and was very careful to ensure that no Santa presents were put under the tree until early Christmas morning when we were all still asleep. I truly believed that Santa Clause put the presents there. I remember waiting up all night long on Christmas Eve trying to peak around the corner of the staircase, only to fall asleep on the floor every single year. I still have no idea who would carry me upstairs to my bed.

I remember waking up on Christmas morning, feeling like the happiest kid alive. The presents were great and all, but it was all the family members that would come over to visit and the great food we would all eat. Everything felt so normal on Christmas day during my childhood years.

Before the Christmas meal would get underway, the mysterious large box truck would pull up in front of our 20 Cedar St home and my grandfather would take us outside in our pajamas. This was the moment, when once a year we would say hello to

Chubby, a short, balding, overweight man with a cigarette in his mouth. He would shake my grandfather's hand and open the rear sliding door to the box truck. Chubby would help my grandfather lift us into the back of the truck and my grandfather would say, "Just one trip, that's it, take what you can carry in one trip!" I would pass by the grown up items and would eventually walk out of the box truck with items like a remote control car or a baseball glove. That is a great memory that still lives with me.

I always took care of those baseball gloves and can remember playing little league baseball like it was yesterday. The best part about childhood baseball was that the field was right down the street from 20 Cedar St. Baseball became the one thing that I really looked forward to every single day. Even though baseball made me feel normal, I can still remember playing on the ten-year-old little league all-star team and doing a few dumb things.

My most memorable little league pastime had to be during the singing of the national anthem, when our team was nicely lined up on the first baseline with our hats to our hearts. For whatever reason, with all the parents and children watching, I decided to turn to my right and give an extremely hard knee to my teammate's outer thigh. The knee was so hard and unexpected, that I dropped him to the ground instantly. He cried on the ground as our nations song continued to play, but worst off, he

45

was unable to play due to the deep contusion in his thigh muscle. The coaches yelled at me for a brief moment but let me off easy, knowing the risks when they accepted me to the team. I don't know why I did these stupid acts of violence, I wasn't a mean kid, maybe just a coward.

About a year earlier in the fifth grade, I had turned around in class just to strangle the kid who sat behind me. I simply turned around and grabbed him with both of my hands from the front of his throat and squeezed. Just as he was passing out, the classroom teacher tackled me off of him. After chaos was restored in the classroom, I was pulled out and sent to the principal's office and asked why I strangled and nearly rendered the boy unconscious. The only answer I had for the principal was, "I don't know." I received a few days off from school for what I had done and had to give the classmate an apology when I returned. Instead of strangling people for a hobby, I continued playing baseball in order to keep myself on the right track.

I ended up becoming a very good baseball player over the next couple of years, and even had a few local scouts come to watch me due to some newspaper articles that I'd been in. I was a pitcher, and a pretty good one for a messed up kid, but I had a serious problem with not getting serious with anything.

I can remember my uncle Vincent visiting one day when I was about twelve years old. He saw me

46

leaving the house and wanted to walk with me to my baseball practice. On our way there, he pulled out a lighter and told me to set some brush on fire. I told him that I didn't want to, but he immediately reassured me to do so. I took the lighter from my deranged uncle and did what he said. The fire then quickly spread over a short period of time and caught onto a small factory which got out of control. The baseball practice was a couple hours long and the field was only about a mile away from the fire. I can still remember watching the black smoke fill the sky as practice went on.

At that point in my life, I started to not care so much about baseball either. My throwing arm was starting to have a lot of pain and numbness around the shoulder and elbow area, due to the curveballs that were required in this fairly competitive baseball town. I couldn't throw the ball for more than a couple innings at a time anymore and realized that something was wrong. One day during the next year's baseball tryouts, I let the coach know about the pain I was having in my throwing arm. The assistant coach said to the head coach, "Well if he can't throw, then what good is he?" I can still remember hearing those exact words, and it really bothered me. Instead of the coach being an adult and maybe asking me what was wrong and possibly trying to help, they just simply said that I was good for nothing, just a couple feet away from me like I was an animal. I got up from the bench, left the

47

field and walked home, never to play a single game of baseball again.

I was so confused with my life at that point that I didn't even know what the heck I was supposed to be doing. I was about thirteen years old, terrified of life, and never felt comfortable with myself. I was shy, scared, nervous, embarrassed, and everything else put together. There were always girls my age wanting to have an emotional teenage relationship with me, but I would just ignore those situations because I didn't know what to do or how to feel. I just wasn't normal and think back to that time, wondering why it had to be that way. I wish I could've done it all over again, and had that exciting youth life like all the other kids experienced. I wish I could've expressed myself in the ways I truly wanted to. I remember kids my age talking about kissing girls and grabbing boobs. I remember trying to change the subject quickly, because I was terrified in the event they would ask me questions about those awkward situations in which I had absolutely zero experience or knowledge of. I had nobody to talk to when it came to girls and relationships, and nobody in my family ever thought it was important to tell me about it. There was nearly no emotion or affection inside the walls of 20 Cedar St, and I can't remember a single time that my grandparents ever made physical contact.

Anyway, it had been a couple of years since Uncle Vincent had moved out of 20 Cedar St and into his new residence. It had been pretty quiet around the house, other than the fact that my brother Tony and Cousin Vincent Jr were doing their normal routine in the basement. They were usually just playing cards, smoking pot, and getting cocked with their buddies. My grandfather would rather have them at home getting boozed up than out in the streets I guess. He would rather have them not touching any of that crap, but at least he had them home where he could check in on them from time to time. When my grandfather would make his way down the basement stairs to give a health and welfare check, they would all hide their beers and weed under the poker table. I still wonder if they actually thought my grandfather couldn't smell the booze on their breath or the weed in the air. It was also very possible that they just hid the junk from him out of respect.

It didn't take long before I was down in the basement as well. At thirteen years old, I was getting drunk too. My brother and cousin would give me three beers and play the song "Roxanne" by the Police. I would then have to guzzle beer every time the song would say "Roxanne." We would normally consume about three beers during each play of the song. I can remember doing this in junior high and even on school nights, getting so tanked that I would barely make it to my bedroom. At times I would throw up at night, on top of my bed, on my sheets, and all over myself. I would sleep in the barf all night long until morning came around, when I would take a shower and go to school. I was such a mess up, but nobody ever told me, so I figured it was alright. I was just trying to fit in with my older brother and cousin, but I wish I had better role models now that I look back.

My cousin and I had begun to hang out more than my own brother and I did around that time. Vincent Jr was so disturbed and I could see it in his eyes. He had an angry look on his face a lot of the time, but you could see the sadness right through it. I think the difference between the two of us was that I was too scared to be angry as a kid.

Just a year or so earlier was a very traumatizing time in my cousin's young life. My aunt Sarah ended up swallowing a bunch of drugs that were fronted to my uncle Vincent from a dealer. My uncle needed to sell those drugs to make a little cash to pay back his supplier and to buy some narcotics for himself. Without the pills and no way to pay back the supplier, my uncle Vincent took his base-ball bat to my aunt for quite a while, turning her into pulp. My cousin was there at the condominium at the time of the beating and tried to stop his dad, but my uncle took the bat to him as well. My uncle Vincent was sentenced to five or ten years in state prison for the savage beating of his wife. After her recovery, my aunt Sarah moved many miles away from the 20 Cedar St area, but the curse still found a way to finish her off, as she later died of cancer at a fairly young age.

My cousin and I were in a very similar boat at that time, as the major contributing factor was that neither one of us had parents. My cousin started to live at the cursed 20 Cedar St home permanently and I was happy to have him there. Luckily for him and the rest of us, we didn't have to be around his evil father anymore. Vincent Jr was always around at that point and would take me in the backyard to play catch with the football, shoot hoops, and go on long bike rides. He started to take me to the gym with him and I started working out at a young age. My cousin was always very good to me.

I can remember years earlier, when my uncle Vincent had smacked me around in his bedroom for taking a few items from his dresser that I had previously stolen for him. I was crying and scared, but my cousin showed up minutes later to the house. He pulled me away from his father, took me outside, and sat me on the handle bars of his bicycle. He pedaled me around the neighborhood until I stopped crying. There were other nights when I would be in my bed trying to fall asleep, when my cousin would show up to 20 Cedar St. He would come up to my room to check on me and scratch my head until I would fall asleep. This very small part of the book was extremely difficult for me to write. My cousin was the closest thing I ever had to a real brother, and I was very close to him. I realized later in life that I loved him more than I ever knew.

Chapter 5

I was a full blown teenager, and remember learning that I did have the ability to make my own choices. I learned that there was a difference between right and wrong, and that I had the power to control every single one of my actions, so I thought.

On one particular day of childhood, I remember my grandfather taking me to school, when he abruptly stopped at a local gas station. He got out of the car and went inside the store to purchase a newspaper. When he sat up and left the vehicles seat, about five dollars in quarters slid out of his pocket, and the money was laying right next to me. I quickly grabbed the money and put it in my jacket pocket like a piece of crap. A minute or so had passed and for the first time in my life I said to myself, "What the hell am I doing?" I was stealing from my grandfather, the man who gave up a lot of his own life to try to raise me. I took the money out of my jacket pocket just before my grandfather got back into the car. He entered the car and sat down. I said to him, "Here Grandpa, you dropped this money on the seat." My grandfather said, "Oh, thanks Jason, you can keep it." It was one of the first lessons that I had ever learned as a kid, that doing the right thing will sometimes pay off, but it always feels good when it's all said and done. I never forgot that day and remember it like it happened yesterday.

Just a few months later in early spring, my grandfather and I were racing on foot from the car to the house with some groceries in our hands. My grandfather would always win and was in pretty good shape for an older man. But on this day, when his foot hit the second step of the front porch stairs, his leg gave out and he fell. I couldn't believe that he fell, he was the strongest man in the world to me and I definitely became nervous. He had a look on his face like he saw a ghost, and then I turned terrified knowing something was wrong, but I didn't know what.

Two weeks later, my grandfather began throwing up blood on the first floor kitchen area of 20 Cedar St and was taken to the hospital by ambulance. It was a few days later that the man who tried to raise me and my siblings had been diagnosed with stage four prostate cancer. The doctors gave him about six months to a year to live. My grandfather was a man who wasn't afraid of anything and kept our dinner table filled with punks like me in check. This was an extremely sad time in my life, but again, I was so traumatized and nervous about everything, that I didn't feel much. I soon became terrified to even talk to my grandfather, just because of the scared coward I was. Years of never discussing our problems at 20 Cedar St had turned me into someone who was extremely afraid to discuss the new situation with my grandfather. I watched him begin to lose weight, hair, and happiness. Instead of him running the house and keeping us all in line, I would only see him lying in his hospice bed at that point. He would cry for much of the day and I was too scared and nervous to stop and talk to him.

It was my grandfather's last Thanksgiving and he was no longer in charge of the family or the dinner table. Vincent Jr pushed him in his wheelchair up to his favorite spot at the dining room table where we had eaten so many holiday meals together. It was the same room and dining table where my grandfather's parents had celebrated many holidays and birthdays nearly one-hundred years ago. It was where my grandfather celebrated his own birthdays when he was just a small child. It was also the room where my grandfather celebrated every special occasion with his own children, and then his grandchildren.

For the first time in all my young life, I didn't sit next to my grandfather that holiday. I was shaking, heartless, scared, and didn't know what to do or say. I sat across the table in a different spot, far away from my grandfather, completely avoiding him out of fear and cowardly emotion. Once everybody was seated, you could hear a pin drop. Coming from the loudest house on the street, this was the first time I can remember quiet like that. Nobody knew what to do or say. Even my grandmother sat there in shock with her lips sealed. Nobody would even serve themselves a single god damn bite of food.

All of a sudden, my grandfather started to cry and then I started to shake like I always did when I got nervous or scared. Luckily my cousin and brother were there. My brother Tony said loudly, "*Forget this!*" They picked up my grandfather from out of his wheelchair and carried him down the flight of stairs, placing him into the passenger seat of his maroon Chevrolet Caprice. This was the first time my grandfather had been outside in months. They took him for a drive around town for a few hours. I don't know what was said or what my grandfather told them if anything, but this would be the last time my grandfather would ever leave the cursed 20 Cedar St home alive. I never bothered to ask my brother or cousin what was said in that car ride or where they went, because that's just not the type of family we were. While they were gone, we cleared off the table and put the food in the refrigerator. Nobody that I can remember had eaten their thanksgiving dinner that year.

I was fourteen years old and it was my freshman year of high school. My brother and cousin had graduated just the year before. Uncle Vincent was still locked up and I hadn't done anything wrong in a while. I actually got myself a job working at my relatives catering business, washing dishes and cleaning the slop off of dinner plates after buffet style parties. It was a nasty job scraping people's uneaten food off their plates and filling up pig slop barrels, but my relative got a few extra dollars from the pig farm for the tub of people's leftovers. It was nice to be working around family at the catering business and I really needed it at that time. My boss was a relative of mine and he always helped us out. At the end of every shift or so, he would give me a jar of melon balls and a large bowl of chicken soup to take home to my grandparents. My grandmother didn't have the energy to cook anymore and we were all on our own.

It was winter and I was still too terrified to approach my grandfather, who would cry or sleep most of the day. He must've weighed about eighty pounds at this time and was full of loose skin. I was still so scared and nervous to be around him, that I avoided him like the coward I was.

One day soon after, I returned home from school and decided to warm up a bowl of soup on the oven. All of a sudden, I could hear someone yelling my name, "*Jason, Jason, help!*" I went to the voice knowing it was my grandfather calling for me. I was so terrified to make contact with him, that I had considered not helping him at all, as if I never heard his call for help. I approached the living room and there he was, laying on the floor in just his boxer shorts. For the first time in about a year, I wasn't afraid to look at my sick grandfather. I rushed over to him and picked up his cancer stricken body. My grandfather, who was two-hundred and thirty pounds no more than a year earlier, was now an eighty-pound bag of bones with skin falling off of him in every direction. I picked up the most important person in the world to me and he had nothing left to him. I placed him back onto his hospice bed which laid in the living room, replacing his favorite light brown sofa chair. I then spoke my first words to my grandfather in a long time and said, "Grandpa what happened?" He told me, "I don't know, I got up to walk and I fell." He then said, "My legs are weak," and asked me what smelt so good in the kitchen. I told him that I was warming up some soup. He then told me that he was starving and asked if I could pour him a bowl, and I did. My grandfather, who hadn't eaten any amount of food in nearly a month, ate the entire bowl of soup. It was as if everything was normal, as if he wasn't even sick, as if he forgave me for being such a piece of crap coward during all that time I avoided him because I was so scared.

My grandfather and I had a conversation for the first time in about a year, and he hadn't really talked to anyone in normal conversation in quite a few months. He would ask for simple things like to adjust his bed, or ask my little sister to scratch his head or to shave what was left of his facial hair. My grandfather had been far too depressed and scared of dying to talk with anyone for quite some time. While my grandfather and I sat there, he asked me if I was still playing baseball and how school was going. He also asked me how my brother, cousin, and sisters were doing and I told him that everyone was great. My grandfather didn't seem to be sick anymore. He was skinny, full of loose skin, and on a hospital bed, but he wasn't sick for that moment. I remember how happy I was for that short period of time. I had my grandfather back, and it is another one of the most memorable moments of my life.

My grandfather told me that he was tired and was going to take a nap, so I covered him with a blanket and allowed him to fall asleep. I then realized that my cancer stricken grandfather was still my grandfather, the man who tried to raise me, and I wasn't scared any longer. I told myself that I was going to take care of him the best I could from that point on. My grandfather slept for nearly the entirety of the next few days, as I remember coming home from school seeing the paramedics pushing him out of the house. My grandmother was holding his hand and loudly said, "*No, No, No, Fresco!*"

The 20 Cedar St curse destroyed my grandfather and took away the first person in my life that I ever truly had feelings for. I didn't realize how much I loved him until many years later. The only thing that remained in his favorite relaxing area of the living room was the empty hospice bed that he died on.

This part of the book was extremely difficult for me to write, as I cried during every stroke of the keyboard. I cannot get this time back to make things right with my grandfather, and that is something that I'll have to deal with for the rest of my life.

The funeral was three days later and it was the last time I would ever see my grandfather's face. I don't know who wrote the obituary in the local newspaper, but they managed to put all of his wise guy nicknames and illegal criminal activity pastimes in it, along with the great deed of raising all of his grandchildren. Many of my grandfather's connected partners attended the funeral, and that was the last time I would ever see them again. I learned soon after the funeral that once you die, not even your criminal business partners come around anymore. They don't check in on your family, they don't help you out, and they definitely don't come over on Sunday mornings anymore like clockwork with a box of doughnuts. Once you are no longer able to make money with your hustling partners, you're as good as dead.

Once the viewing of my grandfather's open casket had come to an end, everybody but immediate family was escorted out of the funeral home. Out of nowhere, two state troopers entered the funeral home escorting a fully shackled man. His head remained down and he began to cry, that was when I realized who it was. Nearly one-hundred pounds lighter and with a clean looking haircut, my uncle Vincent approached his father's casket. He continued to cry, made eye contact with his mother, and was taken back to prison to finish the remaining years of his incarceration. It had been nearly three years since my uncle had beaten his wife to a pulp with a baseball bat, and I wondered if that would be the last time I would ever see him again.

Within a few months, my brother Tony began getting involved in the druggie and hippie lifestyle. This was also the real beginning to the disastrous road he would eventually lead his life down. Luckily for me, I had Vincent Jr living at the 20 Cedar St house while I was going through my first few years of high school. Despite the fact that my cousin was half a psychopath due to the abuse from his father, he still managed to be a real hard worker and always held a job in the construction field. For those who knew him, they understood that he was an extremely loyal friend, and a special character with one of a kind humor.

My best friend lived right down the street and I started hanging out with him even more at this point in my life. He still had the same great parents from back in my catechism days, and they loved me as much as they loved to feed me. It was a nice home to be around and everything was in order, the way a home should be. I was about fifteen years old and can remember a very special day at my best friend's house. His dad loved me like a son and believed that I was old enough to give me his condolences about the death of my mother. He said to me, "Jason, I'm sorry about what happened to your mother, it was a tragedy, she was a beautiful woman." It was the first time in my life that anyone had ever tried to console me or even mention the death of my mother. I said back to him, "Thank you, she burnt her arm pretty bad from the barbeque fire, right down to her veins and died." His eyes got so big you would've thought he saw a ghost. He changed the subject quickly and went back to eating his dinner. I could tell that he was blown away by something that I'd said about my mother dying. I knew at that point there was something was very suspicious about my mother's death, but I was still too scared and shy to ask him any questions.

Chapter 6

At this point in my life, summer vacation from school wasn't a big deal anymore. School break wasn't the same as my younger years, when I used to look forward to those beautiful childhood vacations at our family's cottage near the coast. It was told to me that my grandfather had gambled away the deed to the family vacation cottage a few years before he died.

I was entering my sophomore year in high school and most of my friends had their own cars, pocket money, and came from fairly wealthy families. Even though I was definitely jealous of what they had, I never acted that way. They were true friends and really great people. There were definitely a handful of them that would've done anything for me, and I will never forget them.

I needed some money and needed it pretty quick. My brother Tony was back in town for the winter and was working at an outdoor Christmas tree store about ten minutes from 20 Cedar St. I asked him if he could get me a second job working with him a few days per week. He put in a good word and ended up getting me the job where he would sell Christmas trees and tie them down to the customer's vehicles.

On my first day of work, we entered the parking lot looking for a spot to park our vehicle. While driving through the lot, a car backed out of its parking space and nicked a microscopic scratch on the rear passenger quarter panel of my brothers passed down and third Chevy Caprice in the family. That was my first and last day of work at the outdoor Christmas tree store. I quickly thought about the possibilities and endless opportunities that came along with filing a lawsuit. The pain from the injuries I had sustained brought tears to my eyes, and I immediately called the police for a report. After the horrific accident, I went to the 20 Cedar St local lawyer's office and told him that I wanted to be represented for my injuries. He took the case and got a copy of the police report. He then asked to see the car so he could take some photos and assess the damage.

The very next day I showed up with the vehicle, and I'll never forget the look on the lawyer's face when he saw the damage. The lawyer met me outside of his office to take accident photos and he actually had to ask me where the damage was. I remember pointing it out to him and said, "Oh, it's that tiny scratch right there." He asked me where the dent was and I told him, "Does there need to be a dent for me to get injured." He looked at me and I could tell he wanted to say, "You lying son of a gun!" My personal belief was, "Since he's a lawyer, he's probably just as hungry for money as me," so I knew he'd have nothing to say. He told me of a great chiropractor and then he gave him a phone call to set me up with my first appointment. Due to my pain and suffering and having to go to so many appointments that year, I must've missed nearly forty half-days of high school, but can't remember exactly how many.

I had nobody around to tell me what to do, and since I had no guidance, I simply did what I wanted. A few months after the chiropractic appointments were finished and my injuries had subsided, the lawyer handed me a nearly four-thousand dollar check for my pain and suffering. I went out shortly after and bought myself a vehicle with my hard earned money. The high school administrators knew my family history as I can recall, so they ended up passing me that school year with the bare minimum across the board. I'm sure that I should've failed nearly every single class, but they did us both a favor and just pushed me through.

After learning how nice it was to earn easy money just like my grandfather had done for so long, I realized that I wanted to continue down that road. I was still a hard worker though and got a job after school, on the weekends, and during the summers with my cousin Vincent Jr doing land-scaping work for a local company. My cousin and I put in a lot of hard work and spent a lot of time together during the summers. I always seemed to look up to him because he wasn't a coward like me.

I went on to look for my next score and found a buddy of mine working at a local neighborhood convenience store. I put together a plot to steal some items in order to help supplement my income. I waited until the days he was working the cash register and I would grab a couple watches from the spinning display case and would place them on the counter as if I was going to pay for them. After that, I would hand my buddy a pack of twenty-five cent chewing gum and he would only ring up the gum. He would run the scanning gun over the watches, but would never pull the trigger, making it look good for the security camera. He would put everything in the shopping bag and I would walk out as if nothing ever happened. I was able to do this about once every week, and would also take Walkman radios, cameras, and items like that. I found a few pawn shops a couple towns away and was able to sell the stolen items for about thirty-five to forty percent of the sticker price. This went on for quite a few months until things got too hot for my buddy, so he took a job with another local business.

The money from the small heists was very good while it lasted. I had a little more cash in my pocket than usual and didn't find myself being so jealous of everyone else around me. I was finally able to buy my own stuff for a while and it sure felt great.

I would only work Saturdays and of course the entire summers with my cousin at the landscaping job. Without my grandfather to help support me anymore and my grandmother surviving off of her social security check, I needed to do what I could to survive. I had researched into a new afternoon job because I had plotted a devious scheme before I even filled out the job application. It was a corner store, but they also did some catering and sold a crap load of beer, that was the lightbulb for me. I was later hired and it turned out to be decent work. They kept me in the pots and pans room for a while, until sometime later when they moved me upstairs to stock beer and supplies onto the shelves.

The time had come and I finally made it upstairs where I had been waiting to be all that time. I came up with an even better game plan after learning the ins and outs of the building. I watched the exact operation of the store, to include who worked what hours and how they worked. After about three weeks, I discovered that the set schedule of the store had left the owner, an old man, in charge of the entire operation a couple evenings a week. My plan was to steal beer when he was working, bottom line. Even if other employees noticed that beer was missing, I believed they would just think that the old man messed up on the register, and who would tell him anything, he was the owner.

I remember being so excited about my newly designed plan that I called up a few friends that I could trust, and asked them to get me some beer orders for the weekend parties. Since we were all under age, I could've sold the beer for two times more than the store rate. Instead, I decided to sell the nice microbrews for slightly more than they were worth, between twenty-five and thirty dollars a case. I began to acquire one case of beer a week, just to see if it would get noticed. I remember telling the old man that I was going to make a dumpster run with the extra-large wheelbarrow that they kept in the back of the store. I would place the case of beer in the wheelbarrow and then cover it with a few bags of the stores trash. I would wheel it out the back of the store and then park the wheelbarrow on the side of the dumpster so nobody could see from inside. Once I was finished throwing the trash, I would take the case of beer and leave it on the ground next to the dumpster. It was fairly dark at night in that parking lot, so nobody could see the beer. I thought to myself, "Even if they did see the beer, why would they think it was a full case, wouldn't it be perceived as just an empty box next to the dumpster." I would then contact a close friend who would pick up the beer from the dumpster area. He would keep a six pack for himself and sell the remaining three six packs at the party for me that very same night. My profit was about a cool twenty bucks or so to add to my nights pay.

To say the least, they never noticed the one case of beer disappearing off the books, so I quickly bumped it up to two and so on, until I was acquiring about three cases a week, which was where I peaked. My regular salary had been earning me about a whopping hundred and twenty dollars a week, but my beer sales had earned me a good supplement on top of it. I was also drinking beers free of charge with the little extra's I kept for myself.

I was doing pretty well for a high school kid, at least that's what I thought. I forgot that I was even doing anything wrong.

One high school day that year, I was called from my classroom to the principal's office and was told to sit down in front of his desk. I had no idea what the principal wanted from me, so I thought maybe it was to tell me someone else in my family had died, or possibly that something horrific had happened at my cursed 20 Cedar St home. I was sitting in the office when the principal took the phone off of hold. He picked it up and said, "Hey Bob, here he is." The principal handed me the phone and I said, "Hello". The nearly fifty-year-old son of the store owner who I had been stealing beer from had begun to dish out all the curse words he could think of. This was one of the greatest fire-works of curse words that still to this day I have ever heard, and it was right there in a public school's principal's office. The store owner's son screamed, *"You son of a gun, you little mother stinker,"* and so on. He then yelled, *"Admit that you've been stealing from me you thief piece of crap, so I can send the police over there and arrest you."* I yelled back with, *"I didn't steal anything from your store."* He then stated that he was going to call the police anyway, and I said, "Call them, you don't have nothing on me, I'm not a thief, and I never stole from you." Well, the police never went because they had no evidence of who was removing beer from the store. Every other worker probably got word of what I may have been doing and snitched me out. With mutual understanding, I never showed up to work again and continued landscaping with Vincent Jr.

The beer had run dry, the money had become pretty tight, and I was itching to do something crooked. I quickly found many new and immoral business opportunities during high school that would help keep money in my pocket. I quickly started to get deeper and deeper into making bad personal decisions in order to make money during this hard time. I have no desire to include the most disappointing personal decisions that I made during this young time in my life. I have no intention on disclosing these acts and simply did what I had to do, realizing later in life that I was no different or better than any of the other men from 20 Cedar St. The only thing that I am proud of, is that I never manipulated family, relatives, friends, or anyone who truly loved me.

Chapter 7

Senior year in high school is supposed to be the best year for teenagers, but not for kids who lived at 20 Cedar St. My older sister had already graduated high school and moved into her aunt's home for a short period, while she prepared to attend college nearly one-hundred miles away. My younger sister decided to stay at 20 Cedar St with me for a little longer. My brother Tony was involved in the possession with intent to distribute business along with theft, and Vincent Jr had just moved out and got his own place to live a few towns away.

My grandmother wasn't doing so well anymore, and it was sad to watch her crumble at 20 Cedar St. She was losing her mind and at the same time surviving off of two things, coffee and cigarettes. She would bring the old stainless steel coffee percolator and place it on the end table next to her reclining chair, along with two packs of Marlboro lights. She would pour a cup of coffee and then light a cigarette to start the day nice and early. After taking the first drag of her cigarette, keeping it in her right hand, she would then grab the coffee with her left. She would then take one sip of the coffee and complain that it was too hot. After about twenty minutes of a "Matlock" television episode, she would snap out of it and realize that the ash of her cigarette was about two inches long and out. She would then go for her second sip of coffee and realize it was cold. She would put out the cigarette in her ash tray and throw the coffee out the window, which was right next to her. She did all that without having to even get up from her favorite chair. My grandmother repeated those steps over and over, all day long, during her last year at 20 Cedar St.

During that year with my grandmother, she would constantly ask me where my mother was, or when my grandfather was getting home. She would say, "Jason, where in the hell is your mother, she left with your uncle Vincent this morning and she hasn't come back yet, I'm really worried!" I would tell my grandmother in the nicest way, "Grandma, she died a long time ago, you don't remember." My grandmother would yell at me and ask me why I would make up such awful things. Sometimes she would get so confused and worried about the situation that she would cry. She really believed that those past events were actually happening at the present time.

She started to hallucinate about other things in the home as well. She would call me over to the living room while sitting in her favorite chair, and would ask me if I could catch the "God *damn chicken*" that kept running around the house. These types of instances went on nearly every day.

I can remember back to these moments right down to the cigarettes being Marlboro lights, but occasionally Misty lights when money was even tighter. I remember these facts exactly, because I had been one of the individuals purchasing the cigarettes for her from the gas station down the street since I was about nine years old.

During spring of that year, we placed my grandmother in an elderly care center down the street, where she was diagnosed with Alzheimer's. I felt bad for my grandmother and later realized, or made my own assumption that she didn't have Alzheimer's as they said she did. Much later in life I came to believe that she lost her mind from the awful secret that I believe she kept hidden inside for many years.

It was only my little sister and I at the cursed 20 Cedar St home and I'm still unaware to this day of who was paying the utility bills, but they never turned off. The home was in foreclosure status, but we kept on living there. Luckily, I always had my best friend's house down the street to feed me when times turned really bad. Without my best friend's family in my life, I would've been forced to continue surviving off of the Salvation Army food I was receiving. Government issued peanut butter, stale bread, and dehydrated vegetables were the only food items stocking the shelves at 20 Cedar St. I will never forget what my best friend's parents did for me for as long as I live.

I continued working with Vincent Jr even though he moved a few towns away. The landscaping office was right down the street from his new rental home, but he would drive twenty minutes to pick me up and drive twenty minutes back to the office on the days I would work with him. He did that on the weekends and every day in the summer. He was truly there for me at that time, but I also think that I was truly there for him as well.

When he would get to 20 Cedar St on Saturday mornings to pick me up, I was sometimes still drunk and sleeping. He would kick the crap out of me in bed and tell me not to be a freaking junkie like our parents were. I would fight off the hangover, get up really quick, and was out the door in seconds. Even though I had a vehicle, he still came to pick me up. He knew me better than anyone and figured I would never show up to work on my own, and at times he was right. I knew he liked having me around because I was someone he could relate to, considering we lived the same life for the most part. We truly spent so much time together that I considered him my brother. I never had that type of relationship with my real brother, and besides, he was gone since I was about seventeen years old when he started his criminal career.

I graduated from high school at the bottom of my class and am grateful today that they even passed me. I was eighteen years old and without a plan. Vincent Jr had recently hurt his shoulder at work and settled for a nearly sixteen-thousand dollar lawsuit. Without him to work with, I didn't feel like landscaping anymore, it just wasn't the same. He moved hundreds of miles away from the 20 Cedar St area and started fresh with his settlement money. I was truly alone and decided to get a real job, believing that it was time for myself to change my ways.

I was offered a job from someone who knew my best friend's family fairly well, doing cement precast work. I started the new job and realized that it was an extremely physical job. After busting my butt for a few months for crap pay, I wanted to steal again. After looking around the building really good, I realized that there was nothing to steal. I truly didn't know what to do with my life at that point. I certainly didn't want to make concrete precast products for the rest of my life. The owner of the store quickly gave me a small raise and even allowed me to bring my dog to work. I could never figure out why he was so nice to me. He then told me that he was getting older and wanted to teach me the business so I could run it for him. I didn't know why he trusted me so much, until one day he decided to tell me. Apparently, he was the best friend of my father and felt bad that he was out shooting up heroin with him in the past. He felt as if he was partly responsible for what happened to my father and the outcome for me and my siblings. I decided that I didn't want his charity and didn't feel like being around him anymore, but I needed to, at least until I could find a new job.

I was completely clueless and had no idea what

to do next, so I started to think about everything and anything. My little sister had just moved into her aunt's house as well, and I was the last remaining person at the cursed 20 Cedar St home. A few days later, I was sitting at home and began to think about that day at my best friend's house. The day when his dad's eyes opened up extremely wide after I had just finished telling him that my mother died from a barbeque accident. I knew that there had to be some sort of better explanation of how she died. Since nobody but my grandmother ever discussed the details of my mother's death with me, I decided to start tearing up 20 Cedar St for some clues. I was going to search the entire house trying to see if the barbeque death story of my mother was the truth. I went straight to my grandmother's belonging's first, which was still the way it was left after she went to the nursing home. I searched the second floor of 20 Cedar St like nobody's business and tore through everything that my family owned. I went through every pair of underwear, every piece of clothing, and every single pocket that I came across. I removed the drawers from all the furniture and searched everything inside and under. I flipped over the couches and even looked under the huge wooden tube television that hadn't been moved in at least twenty years. After about three hours of searching on the second floor, I came up with nothing.

I took the rest of the night off, since I had to get

up at five o'clock in the morning for work. I wasn't giving up though, so right after work the next day I drove home and began searching the basement. I went through everything to include all the floor joists. I thought there would've been something in the ceiling of the basement, maybe a shoebox, but there wasn't. After a few hours of searching with nothing to show, I decided to go to sleep.

I was back to work the next day for another grueling day of shoveling concrete. The big difference was that the work wasn't bothering me anymore since I had some sort of goal on my mind. Thinking back, this search for answers was the first positive goal I ever chased in my life. I finished up work for the day, drove home, and immediately began searching the first floor of 20 Cedar St. The first floor was where my grandfather and evil Uncle Vincent had slept in the past. I searched through every item on that floor and still couldn't find a single thing. I was starting to believe that maybe my best friend's dad had indigestion that night. Maybe indigestion was what I saw, not him reacting to my mother's barbeque death story.

It was Friday and another day at work. The day flew by and I was home by four-thirty in the afternoon. I remember having a purpose that day, and I went up to the third floor bedrooms, which also contained a small unfinished portion of the attic. I tore through that attic from top to bottom. I even searched through the three-hundred or so chewing tobacco spit bottles that my brother, cousin, and their friends would throw into the attics crawl space near the roof, so my grandparents wouldn't find out that they dipped. Not all of the dip bottles had a sealed top on them and it was quite possibly one of the most disgusting encounters I have ever come across. That nasty crap got all over me as I voyaged through the mountain of spit bottles.

I eventually came up with nothing and went with my last resort, the huge three-hundred pound cast iron safe that sat in the attic for many years. The combination lock to the safe had been broken for as long as I could remember, and my grandfather always said that there was nothing in it. I always believed that if there was something valuable in the safe, he would've had a locksmith come and open it in the past. Either way, I decided to start pounding the combination lock on the front of the door with a large rock that I had found in the backyard. I smashed for hours, but I did absolutely no damage to the safe. There was no way that I was going to spend the last of my money paying someone to open the safe. Since there was nothing for me to steal at work, I barely had money to survive, never mind paying a locksmith. With nothing going my way, I had officially given up. I realized that maybe some things are just not meant to be known, and that maybe I was better off just believing the barbeque story that I was told. Maybe my mother really did pass away from the infection she developed from the burn on her arm, why would anyone lie to me? I decided not to go out that Friday night to get drunk with my friends and just went to bed.

I slept in very late that Saturday morning with nothing on my mind, the search was over, zero results. I decided that I was going to head to my best friend's house since I knew I was always invited over to eat. I got up, put my clothes on, and stepped out of my third floor bedroom door. I started to make my way down the flight of stairs, but after taking about the fourth step, my grandmother's wooden trunk was staring directly at me. I never decided to open it in the previous days because I had been through that trunk so many times before, but I guess I had never searched through it. I continued to go down the stairs, then I stopped and said, "I might as well finish the job, who knows." I turned around, walked back up the stairs and approached the low to the ground wooden trunk. I got down on both of my knees, just like people do at church and opened it. There it was, the same old linen and curtains just like before. I removed the linen one at a time until I reached the bottom. I lifted up the last linen from the bottom right hand side of the trunk and found a newspaper, an old newspaper. It was upside down and the back page was facing me. I picked it up, flipped it over, and rotated it. I was nineteen years old, alone, and it was nearly fourteen years after my mother had been killed by a barbeque burn, and I started to read the front page headline. Giuliana Salvino "Murdered."

I remember staring at the newspaper like I had just seen a ghost, the same look my best friend's dad made that afternoon at dinner. I remained on my knees staring at the headline. I then started to read the two-page article which talked about what had happened. The article said that my mother had been strangled to death, stripped of her clothes, and taken into the woods where she was buried in a freshly dug grave. The newspaper article had a few statements from my grandfather who said, "My daughter was a beautiful gem." He went on to say that it was an evil human being who killed his daughter. My grandfather also said, "The killer wasn't a normal person, but an animal." There was another newspaper article from about a week later which was folded inside, where my grandfather stated for the first time ever that his daughter was a drug addict, and blamed "The evil of drugs" for her murder. My grandfather wrote a small section about giving reward money for any information that would lead to an arrest. He also mentioned in the newspaper article that he believed he had a really good idea of who the killer was and pointed the police in that direction.

After reading all that information for the first time, I said to myself, "Why would someone kill the daughter of an extremely well liked and connected man?" Even more so, why would a connected man offer reward money or point finger towards someone as the killer, wouldn't he just have them wacked. After reading the articles, which didn't give any fine details of the case, I decided to finally grow up and ask a few questions to an older distant relative. I asked my relative if my mother's case was ever solved and my relative said that the case was still a cold case. I was then told that the rumor around town for many years was that my mother's killer was found tied up and beaten to death at his home, by an Italian crime family that had a very close relationship with my grandfather. I began asking questions to a few more distant relatives, and some apologized to me for not saying anything about the murder. They had promised my grandparents they would never tell us kids what happened, and they kept their word.

After reading and hearing all of that information for the first time, I had become fairly traumatized. I decided to believe the new story that was told to me, that my grandfather had the real killer wacked. It didn't matter to me that the case was unsolved, to me the killer was dealt with.

I decided to give Vincent Jr a phone call to tell him about what I had discovered. After getting a hold of him, I told him about the newspaper I had found, which revealed my mother's actual death. He was blown away that I didn't know what happened to my mother after all those years. He said, "Holy crap Jason, I would've told you what happened to your mom if I'd known you were still believing Grandma's barbeque story." He also said immediately, "My dad killed your mom." I told him he was nuts, then he loudly told me, "*No really he did, you don't believe me!*" I told him that I didn't believe him and he got very upset at me. My cousin was the only person in the world who believed that his evil father was the killer, so I thought. My cousin told me some stories about how his dad would get high and talk about how he killed his sister, then cry before he would pass out. That was as much about my mother as we would talk about, I was still just a punk kid who really didn't care to get any more of my cousin's fictitious details. Vincent Jr was so messed up in the head and traumatized from his father's abuse, that I didn't know when to believe him or not. He also hated his father, but deep down, I wouldn't like to think that he would lie about something as serious as that, but who knows.

I contacted my brother Tony who was out of state at the time, using drugs, stealing, and following a hippie band. I asked him if he knew how our mother died and he said, "Yah, she was murdered." I told him that I just found out, and that I had believed our grandmothers story about the barbeque burn all those years. He said that he remembered being told the same story as well. He told me that he found out what really happened to our mother when he went to school the week following what was also told to him as a barbeque accident. He said he was asked to write out a math problem on the chalk board. Once he finished, he turned to walk back to his chair and saw a newspaper with a picture of our mother on the teacher's desk, and it said, "Giuliana Salvino Murdered." My brother found out that his mother was killed starring at a newspaper just like me, but the only difference is that he had to do it in front of twenty children and a teacher at about the age of nine.

The story of how I found out about my mother's death is another great example of how nobody at 20 Cedar St ever talked to one another about our problems, or even had general family discussions about anything of importance. I understand what my grandmother was doing by telling us the barbeque story, but the reality was that the lies hurt more in the long run. What else didn't we know about our lives? I continued to believe the story of my mother's killer being wacked by my grandfather's people, just like many others did. I understood and determined on my own that it was no longer a cold case, but a closed case.

After finding the newspaper and contacting family members throughout the day, I still had plans on going to my best friend's house for breakfast, which instead turned into dinner. My best friend's uncle was visiting that day and said to me, "Jason, why don't you join the military?" I didn't even know what the military was, really I didn't. I never paid attention in school, and I never felt comfortable talking to anyone. I look back at myself and realize that I truly was a clueless kid. I have to admit that I was getting a little nervous about life, and that soon I would have absolutely nothing left and nowhere to live. I was about to be booted out of 20 Cedar St and understood that I couldn't afford to live in an apartment on my own, even with the Salvation Army food I was still receiving. I didn't want to keep depending on my best friend's family to feed me either.

I asked his uncle to tell me about the military and he told me just what I needed to hear. He said, "I was in the Military Police and it was the best." He told me stories about smoking hash, stealing beer from underage drinkers, and then drinking it all for themselves. He had me hooked, and I believed that I had found a way to steal and break the law legally. I also recollect back and realize that my best friend's uncle said what he needed to, in order for me to become excited about the military. Everyone knew that I needed to get away from the 20 Cedar St area before I ended up in prison or worse. My best friend's uncle knew what he was doing with the story he told me, and I thank him for that today. I went to talk to a recruiter on the following business day and signed up immediately. I told the recruiter that I needed to leave quickly because I had nowhere to live very shortly. Three weeks later, I left home and was officially a soldier. I think back and truly believe one-hundred percent that my true reason for signing up to serve in the United States active duty military was to be, "Above the law."

It was winter and I was the last and final 20 Cedar St family member of four generations to move out of the cursed home forever. The home was soon foreclosed by the bank and purchased by an investor. 20 Cedar St was later turned into and would stay a three family rental home.

Chapter 8

There's not much that I would like to talk about when it comes to the time I spent in the military, but I will mention some of my off duty activity. After completing basic training, I was shipped off to my first oversees assignment. Getting away from 20 Cedar St was definitely a positive move for me. Growing up, I was always scared and shy, so much that I was even terrified of girls. I didn't know what to say to them and was horrified and embarrassed that I had never slept with a girl or even seen a real pair of breasts with my own eyes. I had been avoiding the subject and the entire ordeal for years, because nobody ever told me about sex, why you did it, or what to do. I had never seen affection before at 20 Cedar St except for a few hugs by my grand-mother.

Oversees in the military was just what I needed, far away where nobody knew me and nobody could judge me. While oversees and as sad as it is for being a good looking guy, I ended up having sex for the first time in my life with a prostitute. I then realized that I wasn't scared of having sex with girls, I had just been embarrassed and shy of something that I didn't understand. Needless to say, that really opened up my mind a bit and I was slowly starting to become myself.

There was no more cursed 20 Cedar St home

around me, no more murdered mother, no more Uncle Vincent, and no more weird life back home. I could do whatever I wanted without being judged, shy, or scared of embarrassment. Nobody knew anything about me and it was great, a fresh start. I started sleeping with whatever women I wanted to, and what a confidence booster it was for me. I began doing what normal people my age did, only I went a little overboard. I developed a nasty mindset, was never shy, and was never embarrassed again in my life.

I spent a year over in Asia, and the only difference between me and the normal soldier was that I was able to manipulate the prostitution business after paying for it just the first time. I loved to take and steal, and that's what I did with Asia's "Not so finest." I became the soldier boyfriend to quite a few prostitutes, or as they called themselves, "Juicy girl's." I promised every single prostitute that I would marry them before I went back to the land of opportunity. This allowed me to sleep with them inside of their tiny studio apartments as much as I wanted, in return for marriage and United States citizenship. I would sleep with each and every one of them for months to come until they would start asking for the marriage to take place. They all wanted to receive their military dependent identification card as soon as possible. At that point, I would tell them that I didn't want to marry them anymore. They would get so furious with me, because the prostitutes were the ones who were sup-posed to be scamming the soldiers, not the other way around.

The whole setup was very simple to me; it was just like stealing. I had a handful of prostitute girl-friends that I would go sleep with on the weekends. I would tell them how much I loved them, talk to them about where in the United States we would live, then screw them. Needless to say, I never took one of those prostitute's home, but they did help my new sick mind pass the time while stationed over-seas. I started to really become myself at that point in my life, the person who I was supposed to be, not shy, not embarrassed, and just a little bit disgusting.

Halfway through the oversees tour of duty, I decided to take some vacation time and wanted to go home to the 20 Cedar St area to visit my dying grandmother. I booked a flight and became very excited to see her. I also wanted for her to see her new grandson, a grandson who was no longer afraid of life.

I arrived back home, got off the plane after a fifteen-hour flight and was picked up at the airport by my best friend. We drove to his house and I dropped off my luggage with plans to immediately go see my grandmother and give her a gift that I'd brought back for her. It was late and about ten o'clock at night when I arrived at his home. A group of my friends heard that I was going to be back in town and were already waiting for me before I had even arrived. They asked me if I wanted to go with them out of state for a couple days to celebrate New Year's, and if so, we would have to leave immediately. I told them that I wanted to go see my grandmother at the nursing home before I left, but they convinced me that it was after visiting hours and I wouldn't be able to see her until the next morning anyway. I truly did have plans to see my grandmother immediately or at least by the next morning. Being right down the street from the cursed 20 Cedar St home had begun to affect my rational thinking. I decided to go on the two-day New Year's trip and planned to see my grandmother when I returned. I was going to ask my friends to drop me off really quick just to see her for a minute, but I had become more concerned about going to get drunk at that point.

I remember meeting some girl during the New Year's party and ended up sleeping with her. My friends noticed I was very different and I'm sure that they only remembered the weird, timid, and very shy me. I had a blast on the trip and we returned home the afternoon of the second day. I was once again extremely excited to see my grandmother, but a day and a half later than I had planned. This was the woman who loved and tried so very hard to take care of me all of those years, and I made her wait for me to finish up a weekend of women and beer drinking.

I arrived back to my best friend's house and I

asked him if he'd let me take his car down the street to visit my grandmother. I grabbed her gift, placed it in the car, and drove to the nursing home which was not even a mile away. With my gift in hand, I asked the front desk clerk what room my grandmother was in and I was on my way.

When I arrived outside my grandmother's room, I bumped into my cousin Hanna who seemed to have glossy eyes. My cousin told me that my grandmother had passed away just hours earlier. My grandmother, who was truly my mother, had passed away that morning, probably at the same time I was finishing up my last morning beer. I was so ashamed and disgusted in myself. It was the first time I had ever been away from my grandmother and hadn't seen her in almost a year and a half. I decided to go get drunk and sleep with some girl, instead of going to see my grandmother who gave up most of her life to take care of me.

I entered inside my grandmother's room and shut the door. I remember looking at her thinking she would open her eyes and talk to me, just so I could apologize to her for being so selfish. I should've been there for my grandmother before she died. She was waiting for me, she knew I was coming home that week to see her, and I never showed up. I never could forgive myself for what I'd done, as I remained in the nursing home room with her and cried. I didn't cry for my grandmother that day, I cried for myself. I was still the same selfish person that I'd been all my life. I had done the same thing to my grandfather and I'd done it once again to her as well. I left the nursing home and drove over to the 20 Cedar St home. I stared at the home for a while, trying to figure out why everything in my life had to be the way that it was. The curse that my grandmother believed in for so many years had forced her to relive and remember the traumatic events of her past. The curse finally removed her memory completely before taking her life away.

Within a few days, my grandmother's funeral and burial took place. She was laid to rest at the 20 Cedar St cemetery and was able to be with her daughter once again. I was surprised that my uncle Vincent didn't attend the funeral, but I guess there wasn't any remaining family to pay his way from prison.

The day after the burial, I decided to stop by my aunt's apartment. She was my grandmother's younger sister, and lived just down the road from 20 Cedar St. I tried my best to help her in any way that I could, realizing at that moment that I never cared about anyone else in this world but myself. After spending some time with my aunt over the next few days, I decided to ask her if she remembered the day my mother went missing. It was the first time I had ever discussed my mother's murder with my aunt and had no idea what to expect from her. I found out immediately that she knew the story very well, almost too well. I could see that she became very angry just mentioning it, but not because of what happened to my mother, because of the person who got away with the murder. She explained to me that she was told by my grandparents not to speak about her true feelings to anyone about the murder. She told me about the day that my mother and uncle Vincent left for the methadone clinic to get their fix many years earlier. My aunt told me that she was eating breakfast at 20 Cedar St with my grand-mother when my mother and uncle left by vehicle to the clinic that morning, which was about twenty-five miles away. She told me that she was immedi-ately concerned when my uncle Vincent returned to 20 Cedar St by himself later in the day. My aunt said to me, "When your grandmother asked your uncle where Giuliana was, he started acting very strange." My aunt then said, "Your uncle's clothes were dirty and he had an intensely evil look upon his face, just like he'd done something very wrong." My uncle had responded to my grandmother's ques-tion, stating that my mother met up with some friends at the methadone clinic and was going to get a ride home with them later in the day.

My grandmother's sister was nearly sixty-five years old when she told me this story, and I could still see the anger inside of her. She then said, "I still believe after all these years that your uncle Vin-cent killed your mother." My aunt believed that my uncle Vincent had killed his own sister, just as Vin-cent Jr believed the same. I ended the conversation

91

which angered her to a level I had never seen her at before. I wanted to spend a little time with my aunt while I was home, so I took her to eat her favorite cod and haddock seafood plate later in the day.

It was the last day of my military vacation and I decided to ask my cousin Hanna what had happened to all the furniture and belongings that had been in my family's 20 Cedar St home for the last one-hundred years. She told me that most of it was given away and some family members took what they could carry. I was disappointed that I was never able to have a single piece of anything my grandparents owned in order to keep a part of them with me, everything was gone. Maybe that's what I got for being a selfish coward and not being there for either one of my grandparents when they were dying.

Before I left the 20 Cedar St area that day, I remember starring once again at my old house for quite some time from the front yard, wondering why I had to be part of my family's cursed home. I once again became bothered about myself for the simple reason that I failed to see my grandmother, as it was the main purpose of my trip home. I left the 20 Cedar St area after a twenty-eight day stay and headed back to my duty station in Asia.

I was back in Asia and it had been a few months since the vacation had past. I received a newspaper article about my father who I hadn't heard anything about since I was two years old. It was an obituary, and his early death had finally come from Hepatitis complications at the hands of the curse and the needle. The article was sent to inform me of his death, and that was all that it did. I didn't even read past the headline, or maybe it was the first sentence before I threw it in the trash. I had absolutely zero emotion from that article or for my father. The only thing to this day that my father is and was to me, is the drug addict who had sex with my drug addict mother many years ago, and that's it. I went on the next day, even the next minute like nothing had ever happened. I didn't give two craps about my father.

Time went by and it was finally time to leave Asia. I received military orders to be placed at a duty station in the United States. Even when the military stationed me in the states, they still managed to send me two-thousand miles away from 20 Cedar St.

I arrived to my new stateside duty station and started working in my military police field right away. I was stuck at the police station working the front desk, which ended up working out just perfect for me.

Almost every day, honest people would turn in items that they would find around the military installation to our lost and found bin, which was located inside of the military police station. Sometimes it was diamond earrings, and other times it was phones or watches. Needless to say, I never added the encounters to the daily log. I

93

simply put the items into my backpack and pawned most of it like in the good old days. I still couldn't fix that part of me, I still liked doing wrong.

Slowly but surely I had become a bit lonely at this time in my life, so I continued sleeping with a new woman every chance I could. I never wanted to settle down with a single woman and didn't like the idea of someone having feelings for me. I guess I was an extremely picky individual, had issues with commitment, and never wanted or allowed anyone to get close to me.

One night soon after, I met a girl that was extremely gorgeous at an upscale night spot. She was with her two girlfriends and three men, who I assumed were at least their dates for the night. I remember standing in the bar area and watching this beautiful girl talk with her date or whoever he was, and noticed that she wasn't too interested in him. I decided to approach the table of six to speak to her and I didn't give two craps about the three guys. I arrived to the table and scooted myself in between the two of them and introduced myself to her, "Hello my name is Jason, nice to meet you." She was shocked that some guy had the courage to break up her date and I believed she liked it. Just at that moment I was waiting to get a bottle in the back of the head, or maybe a knife to the side. To my surprise, all that happened was the three men and two other women told my newly introduced friend, "Come on Linda, let's go." Linda said "No, I'm going to stay and talk to Jason." Seconds later, her date and the rest of their crew became very upset, got up from the table and walked away. I had managed to do all that without getting a scratch on me and was very proud of it at the time. Linda and I talked for a while. I told her that I wasn't from the area and had been in the military for a short while. She told me that the guy she was with that night was just an old friend. Linda told me that she was actually in a long term relationship with someone and they planned on getting married.

Later in the night, I asked Linda for her phone number. She told me "No," and replied that she'd already explained to me that she was in a relationship. I was infatuated by her looks and there was no way I was going to take no for an answer. She refused to give me her number, so I insisted that she should take mine in case things with her boyfriend didn't work out. She didn't hesitate to take the number, but I thought she'd just throw it out her car window when she drove off. I walked her to her car, we hugged, and said goodbye.

After a few weeks, I believed that Linda trashed my phone number, so I completely forgot about her. I was a bit hurt, because she was the best looking girl that I'd ever met and believed that the chances of meeting another with her looks would take years. About a month later and out of nowhere, I received a phone call from Linda. She had broken up with her boyfriend and we talked for a long time that day.

95

We began dating shortly after and really did grow to like one another. I became so excited about Linda, that I gave her one of the better pairs of diamond earing's that I received from the police desk as a first gift. I never told Linda the real way I acquired the earrings, so I would only imagine that she thought I bought them for her. I enjoyed being around Linda and respected the fact that she wouldn't let me sleep with her right away.

After about a year of dating Linda, I realized that I didn't like living in the military barracks, due to my lack of privacy. I didn't feel comfortable living around a large amount of people in general anyway, so I rented an apartment out in the city. It was very difficult for me to socialize with ordinary people, and it would sometimes just upset me to see that they were happy and came from a nice family.

I was finally on my own and didn't have military sergeants inspecting my living quarters any longer. I decided to continue my same old criminal-like lifestyle, just like all the men from 20 Cedar St did. I had spiraled out of control this time and went on a five year bad personal decision spree. I was no different or better than my brother or Vincent Jr, just a very lucky individual who never got caught. I thought to myself years later, "Why was I put on this earth, certainly not to behave like a criminal, but why was I so lucky to continue being a free man?"

One day, just months after I had moved into my

new apartment, Vincent Jr called me on my cell phone asking me to go meet up with him at a local casino. I wondered why he would ask me to meet up with him, since we lived roughly two-thousand miles away from each other. I thought he was kidding around, but I soon realized that my cousin was just a few interstate exits away. I was able to break away from the military early that day and went to meet up with him at the casino he had stopped at. Once I arrived at the casino, I knew it was going to be a bad situation from the start, especially after seeing him bet every penny that he owned on a single hand of poker. He lost the hand and I was now placed into a bad financial situation. He broke away from the poker table, gave me a hug, and was very excited to see me. I asked him, "Why in the hell are you here, something happened didn't it?" I soon found out that my crazy cousin had burnt some gambling bridges and owed a big debt to some big people. He also hadn't made a payment on his car in about a year and was running from the repossession man. He needed a place to stay and hide out, and also a little family around that understood him. I was happy to see him, but fully knew the consequences of having him around. I knew that his stay would only put fuel on the fire that I had already started with my own criminal-like behavior.

I can remember one day during his stay with me very clearly. He wanted to go out to a local night club just days after moving into my apartment. I knew there would be consequences being around him, but I have to admit, I loved my cousin. He was always there for me when we were kids and I couldn't turn my back on him. We went out that night to a newly opened night club and I was extremely hesitant about the situation from the start. From the first moment we entered the building, my cousin had begun eyeballing the largest bouncer in the club, wanting to show me that he could kick the crap out of him. I told him to relax and to not draw attention to us.

Later in the night, we were standing on the second story balcony of the club and he said to me, "Hey Jason, check this out!" My cousin proceeded to hock up the biggest loogie imaginable. He then began to slowly drip it out of his mouth with the full intension of dropping it on the bald head of the large bouncer who was standing directly below us on the first level. With pinpoint accuracy, he managed to land this enormous loogie directly onto the bouncer's bald head. My cousin could've easily walked away after dropping the loogie on his head, but it wasn't just a simple prank for him. Vincent Jr just stayed there, and right away I thought to myself, "Oh crap!" The bouncer wiped the spit off his head, turned around, and looked up. My cousin waived up his arms and yelled, *"Come on, let's go!"* The bouncer probably hadn't seen this type of behavior before and became slightly nervous. He scooped up the entire security staff and Vincent Jr and I were in the fight of our lives. I guess they had some respect for my cousins no fear attitude, because the security staff never called the police. They settled for a good night of fist throwing before we were eventually thrown onto the outside pavement. I lost my cell phone in the brawl that night and told Vincent Jr that he needed to stop his ridiculous behavior immediately.

I remember another day while Linda was visiting at my apartment, but was hanging out in a different room than my cousin and I were in. Vincent Jr said to me, "Jason, go for a walk so I can screw your girl, so I can show you that she really isn't interested in you." He said he was going to do me a favor, to show me that she was probably just some whore. Knowing the problems he had, I tried to break it to him gently. I told him that I actually liked her and wasn't going to let him rape her or do whatever he was thinking of doing. I told him he needed to calm down if he wanted to continue staying at my place.

I had been feeding my cousin and was out of money, which forced me to bring in a military buddy of mine to live at the apartment to help pay the rent. After only a few short weeks, I woke up to my new roommate abruptly screaming. My roommate was awoken at about two o'clock in the morning to my cousin staring at him nose to nose, startling the crap out of him. I ran over to the bedroom, grabbed Vincent Jr, and asked him what the hell he was doing. He had tears in his eyes and didn't like the fact that there was someone living in the apartment who came from a nice family. He also said that I upset him for recently correcting his behavior, so he thought about hurting my well-mannered roommate.

The next day, I received a call from my military commander who was told about the incident from my new roommate. My military captain told me that I had two days to move back into the military barracks unless my cousin got far away from me. Vincent Jr had nowhere to go, but I didn't want to go back to the military barracks. I spoke to my cousin about the situation and he understood he screwed everything up. Without a job and nowhere to go, I decided to give my cousin four-hundred dollars, just enough money to drive back to the 20 Cedar St area. My cousin cried in front of me that day and I would deeply miss him, regardless of his crazy behavior. Maybe my cousin not being there was for the better, but I didn't know it would be the last time I would ever see him again.

Chapter 9

My military enlistment was finally over and I was honorably discharged. I had enjoyed competing in numerous military competitions similar to war games and triathlons, which had to do with my extremely high level of physical fitness. I was always well known as a high caliber soldier on the military base, but of course kept my off duty lifestyle to myself. I was offered a job doing security work at the same military duty station, but as a civilian employee. I thought about the idea of doing more security and law enforcement work, but I wasn't very interested. It was somewhat of a conflict of interest for me at the time. "How could I have been involved in security work for a law enforcement department if I was still behaving like a criminal," I thought to myself? I had no other immediate options and needed to pay the bills somehow, so I accepted the position and stayed far away from 20 Cedar St.

Due to the bad personal decision lifestyle I was living, I decided to split up with Linda and went my own way. She wasn't happy that I left her, but with her good looks, I knew she'd be able to move on easily. I was making poor choices at the time and didn't want her to be around any part of it. I actually encouraged her to go find her old boyfriend that I had taken her from before, since I heard he was a decent guy. I was tired of listening to Linda always trying to tell me to change my ways, and I certainly didn't want her to be a part of my bad behavior.

I still had a hard working mentality and wanted to start making more money. I always seemed to have an interest in fixing up homes, but didn't know a darn thing about it. I decided to begin house hunting the very next week and bought my very first home. I put a nice down payment on a beautiful, almost three-thousand square foot fixer upper. The home was in one of the city's up and coming neighborhoods, and I was lucky enough to purchase it at an inexpensive price.

I began educating myself to remodel and repair. I put about ten-thousand dollars into materials and many months of my own hard work into repairing the home. Without Linda, I began bringing my weekend girlfriends around to have my way with them. I realized that I had been having sex with so many women for the past five years, that sex started to become a horrific event for me. I was at a point in my life where I refused to let my weekend girls even touch me when I would sleep with them. Not being touched got me by for a while, but soon enough I was pouring bleach over my body after sleeping with all these women. I felt as if I needed to wash off the nastiness that I believed was all over me. I guess that I had become extremely disgusted with random women sex over the years. Sleeping with so many women in such a fast period of time had begun to sicken me. I actually began scrubbing myself with bleach anywhere on my body that made contact with these women, but especially my genitals. Even though I was cleansing with bleach, I would still keep sleeping around. I think that I was just extremely lonely at this time and of course, a selfish person. I really did miss being with just one woman, Linda.

I hadn't spoken to Linda in almost a year and still respected the fact that it took me so long to get to sleep with her, she didn't give it up right away like almost every other girl I was with. I decided to give her a call and surprisingly she was not in a relationship with anyone, so we were able to pick up where we left off. I believed that she really loved me at that time and we began seeing each other again. I thought that I was truly ready to settle down with Linda after the bleaching episode which lasted for several months. I then thought to myself, "Am I ready to settle down, am I truly willing and able to get away from the criminal-like lifestyle I'm so accustomed to?" I was pretty darn sure that I wanted to be with Linda, but I wasn't certain that I could stop my criminal-like behavior.

I continued to remodel the house and Linda would come over often, spending a lot of time with me. In the next couple of months, I even spoke about marriage and the house being ours. She then began walking around the empty house and started to explain how she would decorate it, and where

103

she'd place certain types of furniture. I began to question myself and wasn't sure I wanted to settle down any longer. I guess you could call it cold feet, or maybe just the inability to allow myself to be loved. I started acting differently towards Linda, until one day shortly after I approached her and said, "I made another mistake, I don't want to get married, and I'm not ready for anyone to move into my house." I told her that I was probably just going to sell the home. I just couldn't do it; I couldn't share myself with anyone on a permanent basis. Maybe it was some sort of defense mechanism from my childhood life experiences, or maybe I was just some weirdo. Bottom line, I told her I was truly sorry for even getting her hopes up and mentioning the idea of marriage. I realized that I was still a horrible, selfish, confused person, just like the kid I had always been. Once again, she was out of my life just like that.

The home turned out to be so beautiful when it was finished, and I remember being so proud of myself for doing something of a good nature for once in my life. When I sat back and looked at what I had accomplished, I realized that I had absolutely nobody to share it with, I was truly all alone. My brother Tony was still in prison, and my cousin Vincent Jr had been doing his own thing, to include prison time for assault and battery. There was no mother to call, no father or grandparents to reminisce with, just loneliness in a big beautiful house a few thousand miles away from 20 Cedar St.

As time went on, I sat back and thought more and more about Linda, deciding to give her a call once again, unsure if she would even pick up the phone. It had been more than a couple of months since we'd last seen each other and I had really hurt her. Luckily for me, her phone number had gone unchanged and she answered the phone immediately, even after what I did. I could hear how excited her voice was on the other end of the line. I told her about how I made a few positive changes in my life in the recent months. I also wanted her to come see the finished home which was a major accomplishment for me. Linda loved me so much that she actually went to my remodeled home that day. I asked her what she'd been up to and she told me that she had decided to make things work out with her ex-boyfriend, the one I kept suggesting she'd go back to. She said that she loved him but wasn't in love with him. She then said, "I'm obviously still in love with you." I told her that I loved her too and I was ready to make a commitment, and wanted to start taking our past relationship more serious if she was willing to be with me one more time. I was so infatuated by her looks that I had to be intimate with her right away and didn't care about her boyfriend. I decided for the first time in my life to let my guard down and leave my future in someone or something else's hands. I decided to sleep with her right then and there, rolled the dice, fifty-fifty shot, whatever happens is what's supposed to happen. With tension, excitement, fear, and whatever else I felt, I decided to let myself go inside of her. I couldn't make up my own mind, but I knew that Linda and I were still truly in love, and allowed fate to decide our future.

Once finished, she became upset and felt as if I was lying to her and messing with her emotions once again. She knew me fairly well and felt as if I had just manipulated her back into bed. I didn't deny her allegations about the fact that I may have just slept with her out of selfishness, and I definitely didn't say anything to make her feel better about what I had just done. She asked if I was serious about being with her again and I just stayed quiet. She said that it was over between the two of us and I believed she meant it. She walked out the door and I just stood there knowing that I was in love with her, but never cared to stop her from leaving. Over the next couple of days, I tried contacting her, but I guess she was really serious about what she'd said. I became very upset and disgusted with myself for treating Linda the way that I did.

Without Linda around, I decided to continue with my bad personal decision lifestyle and went back to my normal routine. I felt like I had to learn the difficult way all the time and never felt comfortable telling anyone my true feelings. No matter how much I loved Linda, I could never actually allow myself to love her or even accept the love she tried to give me. I look back and wish I would've received some sort of counseling during this time as a young adult.

Chapter 10

Months had gone by and I was still living in my big empty house, which had begun to take a toll on me. I had become very lonely once again. After receiving so many compliments from the neighborhood residents about my remodeled home, I decided to sell it. I knew that I would make some money from the hard work I put in, and came up with the idea of moving far away. I thought about moving back home, somewhere in the vicinity of 20 Cedar St. I quickly decided that it was probably too risky to be that close to the cursed home, so I moved onto another idea. I had been getting away with my bad personal decisions and behavior for so long, that I believed I would end up in some sort of trouble if I resided in the vicinity of the cursed home.

I decided to sell the home by owner. After a few months, the home had sold and I nearly made a forty-thousand-dollar profit. I took my money and started applying for security jobs in an ocean front city about seven-hundred miles away. I didn't want to do security work anymore, but it was all that I was qualified to do on paper. I decided that getting away was the best thing for me at the time. It would be a place where nobody knew me or the person that I had become. It was another fresh start and the possibility for myself to change.

After another few months of waiting, I received

a phone call explaining to me that I was accepted for employment from one of the jobs I had applied for. I had about ninety days to report to my new job near the ocean. Even though I was selfish, I knew that I would deeply miss the only woman that I had ever fallen in love with, Linda.

The day before I left for good, I gave Linda a phone call with the hopes of apologizing. She actually answered the phone and I asked if I could see her one last time before moving away for good, just to say goodbye and nothing more. She agreed and said she'd meet me at a local store parking lot which was close to the side of town she was living on. We met up shortly after and I told her that I was sorry for everything. I explained to her that I wished I was a different person with the ability to show emotion. She understood and cried, knowing I was about to leave forever.

It was the first time I had seen or spoken to Linda since the time I slept with her, so many months earlier at my remodeled home. I then noticed that she had a large ring on her finger and was finally married. She seemed somewhat happy with life and her new husband, the same guy as before. Hiding behind her new wedding ring was a look that allowed me to see that deep down inside, she just wanted to be with me. I told her that I sold my home and gave up most of my criminal-like lifestyle. I let her know that I was leaving the next day and that she would probably never see me again. She told

109

me that her husband and herself just had a baby boy together, and the child had been born just two weeks earlier. She began crying, because she knew that any chances of the two of us having children and getting married ourselves was long gone. I was very saddened to hear that she had a child from another man, but it was my own choice to let her go so many times. Linda cried some more, gave me a kiss, and I went in a different direction far away.

I arrived at my new security job and soon bought a small home just off the ocean. With a fresh start at life again, I was almost able to stop my criminal-like behavior. Everything was going great for me at that time, but after a few short months I had become lonely again. I refused to make any friends and normally didn't like to anyway. I had only been living in my new ocean destination for a short time and had already thought about moving again. I thought about the possibility of returning to the 20 Cedar St area once again, despite the curse. I felt like I didn't fit in anywhere else and wanted to be around my family and childhood friends. I began applying for a few jobs in the 20 Cedar St area, because I didn't know where else I belonged at that point in my life. I had begun to think a lot about 20 Cedar St while I was alone in my new home. I started to think about all the immoral things I had done in my life, and I also discovered that I had been lonely since the day I was born. I had also been unhappy since the day I was born, and

110

extremely disgusted with the person I had become over the years. All the immoral and bad personal decisions, the lies and sex with random women, and all the criminal-like behavior. I was still ashamed of myself for being a selfish coward when my grandfather was sick. I thought about the times when I would avoid him because I was scared and emotionless. I was disgusted in myself for never saying anything to my drug addict uncle when he would go on his drug withdrawing rampages. It didn't matter to me that I was just a little kid when those incidents occurred, I was ashamed of myself for not reacting like an adult would've. The piece of crap I was for getting drunk, instead of seeing my dying grandmother. Most of all, I was disgusted with myself and my entire family for never talking or opening up to each other. We were all raised to keep to ourselves and not tell anyone about our problems, just to deal with them. I was disgusted that I couldn't remember ever saying the words, "I love you," to anyone in my family when I was growing up.

I held in all my problems for so many years, that finally my emotions went off like an atomic bomb. I went into an emotional crying frenzy like nobody's business. The crying issue that I began to have was happening everywhere and anywhere. This was no little tear up, and I was crying like an infant who had gone far too long without his bottle. These episodes would approach me all of a sudden and I would try to control them, but I couldn't. I remember anticipating the crying as it would begin to tear my eyes at places as awkward as the grocery store. I would leave my shopping cart in the aisle and take off running to my truck. It didn't matter that I had privacy in my vehicle, I would find myself crying for quite some time. Shoppers would pass through the parking lot and would look at me as if I was some kind of psycho. I can even remember a few crying episodes at work, which forced me into the restroom stall for quite a while. I had begun to realize that I had some alone time in the morning on my drive to work. My brain adapted and I began crying on my morning drives to the office. Certain employees at work could notice my glossy eyes once I arrived, but I had told them that it was just bad allergies.

These crying episodes went on for about six months and I cried like an infant almost every day for at least ten minutes or so, and in the most awkward places. I felt like the crying episodes really did help me and I started to accept my childhood and adult acts of scumbag behavior. This was a life changing moment for me and I felt like I had yet again, another new beginning.

It had been about five months that I had been living away from Linda in my new home in the ocean city. I started to hear back from the few jobs that I had applied for months earlier around the 20 Cedar St area. I was actually offered a few jobs and accepted the better position, having to soon leave and arrive back to my childhood location within a few months. Before I set to return back to the area of the cursed 20 Cedar St home that was responsible for destroying my family, I wanted to get a hold of Linda to let her know again how truly sorry I was for my previous behavior. After all of the crying, I felt like I was better able to communicate with people and open up about myself. I even started to appreciate comedy and began joking around with people for the first time in my life.

It was time for my farewell phone call to Linda and I hoped that she would once again have the same phone number. I decided to give her a call during working hours, because I didn't want to get her in a bind with her husband. She actually answered the phone quickly and we talked for a while. I told her that I was offered a job near 20 Cedar St and that I'd finally be going home in a few short months. I told her how happy I was for her and asked for her email so we could keep in touch, but simply as friends. I wasn't ready to remove her from my life completely and wasn't able to dismiss the fact that she was the only woman from a sexual relationship that I ever cared about. I also gave her my email and we finished our telephone conversation, Linda had a family and I envied it. Maybe it had been all the recent crying and acceptance that brought me to the point of envying a family life. I truly wanted to start being a better person and decided to try living an honest lifestyle.

A few days went by and I emailed Linda, asking her to send me a picture of her son. Her son had to be about six or seven months old by then and I was just curious to see him. Linda emailed me a photo and when I saw the picture I was blown away. The image that I received was very similar to the baby picture's I had of myself, right down to the colored eyes, light hair, and eye shape. I thought back to the day when I slept with Linda, rolled the dice and released inside of her at my remodeled home. I started to add up numbers and said to myself, "*Holy Crap!*" It had been about fifteen months earlier when I slept with her, and the child looked just like me. I wondered if she knew, since her husband didn't have colored eyes or light hair, and neither did she. He was a wealthy man who was fairly short, had dark hair and brown eyes. I let a little bit of time go by, but all I could think of was the possibility that I had a son with the only woman I had ever fallen in love with. I thought to myself and said, "If it's true, I can't allow someone else to raise my son, he might be affected by the 20 Cedar St curse."

I finally decided to call Linda and hinted to her that I thought the child looked a lot like me. She tried to deny it and gave reasons why he wasn't my child. She told me that she'd already considered the possibility of him belonging to me but the time frame was off by a couple of weeks or so. I believed at that moment she'd forgotten about the love she once had for me, now that she had begun living her new wealthy lifestyle with maid service. She also didn't want to hurt her husband's feelings again and I could understand that as well. The guy spent thousands of dollars on beautiful vacations for her, put a monster rock on her finger, and was in the belief that he had a child with her. I believe Linda also tried denying the facts because his wealthy family took her in and treated her like a queen, or maybe she really didn't know that I was possibly the father of the child. I also guessed that she didn't want to become embarrassed, treated differently, or be looked down upon if it were to be true. I understood the way she'd feel if the child didn't belong to her husband. I realized that it would destroy her relationship with him and her in-laws, and they would never feel the same about her again. I thought to myself, "If they disowned her, would I be there for her and the baby," and once again I wasn't sure.

I took some more time with the situation and said to myself, "I would like to become a father who could watch his son become successful, honest, and not a criminal like the rest of the 20 Cedar St men have always been."

I called up Linda and told her that I really wanted a DNA test on the baby. She cried and cried, then yelled, "*He's not yours*!" She said again that the doctor had assured her of the date when she had become pregnant and was able to eliminate me as the father. I told her that I still loved her and if the child turned out to be mine, we could finally be a family. I could tell she was very hesitant of my statement though. She was married, and probably never could forget the times I'd deceived her in the past. Over the next few weeks, she had finally agreed to take the DNA test and said that she'd have to make her husband aware of the situation. I quickly stopped her and explained that I didn't want to disrupt her life. I asked her to just take the DNA test, and if he turned out to be my child, she could then do what she wanted. I then told her that if it turned out I wasn't the father; she could go on with her life as if nothing ever happened.

I explained to Linda that I had become a different person and that I would love nothing more than to have her back in my life with a son of my own. I knew, or at least I felt deep down inside that Linda wanted nothing more than for the child to be mine. It was a few weeks later that I flew back to Linda's home town and she was waiting for me at the airport with a roughly seven-month old boy in her arms. Linda seemed so happy to see me, and it had been quite some time since I'd seen her last. She followed me to the inexpensive hotel that I was staying at, and I'm sure she was quickly able to notice that I didn't have the money her husband had. Even though, I could sense that she was still very in love with me.

The DNA specialist arrived on time to my hotel

room and took our samples. Since Linda was married, I didn't want to spend any time with her and I definitely wasn't trying to be that type of dirt bag anymore. I noticed that she wanted to be around me, at least just to talk, but I was on the road to recovery, and told her that I didn't want to be around her or the child until I got the results of the test. I flew back to my security job the very next day and waited for the results.

A week went by and I received a phone call from the DNA laboratory. The specialist told me that they had the results and asked me if I would like to hear them over the phone or if I just wanted all the paperwork emailed to me. I told them to email it to me and to please stay on the phone so I could read it and ask any questions about how to interpret the results. The email arrived seconds later and I asked the lady where the results were located. I found the section of the findings and read them out loud to the DNA specialist over the phone. In simple terms, the results stated the following, "The likelihood of Jason Salvino being the father of the listed child is ninety-nine point nine percent likely," making it easily understandable that I was indeed the father. I ended the call immediately with the specialist and could feel my heart beating erratically. Once I got myself together, I called Linda and gave her the results. She cried and responded to me in disbelief. She said, "You're lying to me." She still didn't believe me, so I emailed her the results. She then said that she wanted a DNA test by blood, because she had recently heard that a cheek swab wasn't the most accurate.

I got on an airplane a week later to get her the results she needed in order for her to be satisfied and relieved. I got the same company to take another DNA test by blood to make her feel better and also for the results to hold up in court. About a week after the blood tests were taken, I received the identical DNA results as before. She then became afraid and concerned that her husband would try to hurt or even worse, murder her. I was sure about what I wanted and let her know that if she would take me back, we would finally be a family. I gave her my word, which even I knew wasn't much to her at the time. Linda knew that I was unstable with my decisions, but she was still in love with me. I told her to go to her sister's house in order to be safe. I told her to break the news to her husband over the telephone or even in his presence, but at her sister's house with her family around for safety purposes.

It was Thanksgiving week and an emotional one for many. Linda finally told her husband the news and he said that he would take a DNA test of his own. He said that he didn't care if the child was his or not, he still wanted to stay a happy family. Once again, that was the reason that I always told Linda to go back with that guy every time I left her. With the true love Linda had for me, she immediately moved out of her husband's home against his wishes. With the help of her family, she packed her belongings and moved into her sister's home.

I suddenly remembered about the fact that I was supposed to be moving back to the 20 Cedar St area to start my new job. I wasn't going to leave Linda, so I cancelled my newly accepted employment position. I realized that I needed to return back to Linda's home town and began applying for security and law enforcement jobs immediately. I was quickly hired working as a law enforcement officer and would arrive back to Linda and my son within a few months. Right then and there I realized I permanently needed to be a good, honest, and ethical person for the first time in my life. I had three major tests approaching me. First, was I going to be able to stay in a relationship with Linda? Second, was I going to be a good father to my son? Third, was I going to be able to completely and permanently stop my criminal-like behavior? I didn't want to continue making horrible personal decisions just like all the men from my families cursed 20 Cedar St home had always done.

During the few months I had waited until I was able to permanently move back to Linda, her husband had already received and read his own DNA results. It was once again determined that the child was not his. He decided to hire a hot shot attorney to slow the process down and was trying to convince Linda to stay with him. He didn't care if the child was not his, he just wanted to be with the two of them. Linda believed that I wouldn't leave her because I normally would've separated myself from her by then, just like I had done so many times in the past. I told her that I finally had something in my life worth living for, a family. She filed an annulment to their marriage and they were split up officially.

I was back with Linda and my new son, and vowed to be a good, honest, and caring person for the rest of my life. I bought another fixer upper home and we moved in. By that time in my life, I was so happy to be with the only woman I ever fell in love with, and promised myself to never leave her again. The thought of being with the only woman I ever fell in love with for the rest of my life was great. No more random women on the weekends who I couldn't give two craps about. There were no more bleaching episodes deemed necessary and I was happy to not live that life anymore. I was going to be around to watch my son grow up and I promised myself that I would never break the law again.

Chapter 11

It was the second week with my new family and I had a son to get to know. I finally had a real responsibility for the first time in my life. I knew that Linda and my son really counted on me to be there for them. I was going to take care of my new family, unlike the way my parents took care of me. This part of my life is when I became an adult. I had started to become, "America's model citizen," but of course I still had criminal urges that I had to continue to overcome.

I started my new law enforcement job and it was very different from the work I had conducted before. I felt as if I didn't fit in and also felt like a criminal around all of the officers. I started applying for other jobs immediately after feeling that way, but I soon realized that I did fit in and needed to be there more than anyone. I was no better than any of the convicts I was around, just lucky my whole life. It was at that moment, I completely realized that I was no better than my father or my mother. I discovered that my brother Tony and Vincent Jr were just like me and I was just like them. I became very grateful of the luck that had always surrounded me. I was given so many more chances and many more years to grow up and mature than many of the men in my family. I was allowed the opportunity to change my ways with a clean history behind me. This job had taught me to appreciate the fact that I was given multiple second chances in life and showed me where I could've ended up. My new job was another one of the greatest things to have ever stepped into my path, allowing myself to have another daily reminder of how not to behave. I began to appreciate my freedom more than ever.

I loved Linda, my son, and my new healthy lifestyle. I started to truly love doing right and even enjoyed the feeling of pulling up next to a police officer in traffic and waiving, telling the officer to have a great day. In the past I would make it a point to never pull up next to a cop car, I would always stay behind. It was truly a great feeling to have a clear mind. I was clean as could be, looking out for my family, myself, and my career. I never thought that abiding by the law would make me feel that great.

Shortly after, Linda became pregnant with our second child and we finally married one another after quite a long journey. It was spring, and my wife had given birth to our daughter. I had my second child and even more responsibility, allowing myself to fully understand consequences to a whole new level. I knew if I messed up, I'd be leaving my wife and children stranded just like my parents had done.

It was late summer, just a few months after the birth of my little girl, when we decided to look into purchasing a larger home for our growing family. After looking at multiple homes, I finally put a contract on the closest thing to our dream home that my salary would allow. The contract went through and we moved into the home in early fall.

The transition into the new home was back breaking. The backyard was filled with years of debris, scarcely raked or cleaned by the previous owner. After getting all of our furniture in place, I had begun to rake and clean up the backyard so my kids would have somewhere to play outside. While raking, I came across the only item left behind from the previous owner. Hidden under ten inches of leaves and debris was a spading fork. It was the exact type of spading fork I remembered stabbing my sister in the foot with as a child. The same type of spading fork as the one at 20 Cedar St that hung in the garage where my uncle Vincent parked his car for years. For whatever reason, the spading fork had returned into my life. I decided to keep the spading fork in case I could use it around the yard, so I hung it outside and forgot about it.

Months went by and the warm weather of spring had come along with it. Linda and I found out that she was pregnant once again with our third child on the way. Before we knew it, Thanksgiving week was spent in the Hospital and my wife had given birth to our third child, a boy.

I was extremely happy to be a husband and father of three beautiful children, but still missed my 20

Cedar St family very much. I was having a hard time accepting the fact that I had separated from the only life that I had ever known. I guess I felt like a wounded soldier in combat, leaving my fellow comrades behind. I missed Vincent Jr, my brother Tony, and my sisters, understanding how tough it must've been for them all those years. I don't know why, but even though I had a wife and kids, I still felt very alone. I just couldn't let go of my past, realizing that I needed to find out more about it, and clear away all the lies and unanswered questions that I had. I wanted to finally sit down and talk to the cold case investigators who were actively working my mother's murder from many years earlier. Over the years, I had become more bothered about the unsolved death of my mother and the lies that I had been told by my grandmother. I decided to begin clearing away one past experience at a time.

It was just a month after the birth of my third child when my wife noticed that I was acting very strange. My wife told me that I was going nuts, so I explained to her that I really needed to get some answers about my mother's murder and clear my mind. I wanted to hear the facts of my mother's cold case straight from the horse's mouth. I booked a flight back to the 20 Cedar St area and scheduled an appointment with the cold case investigators. It was the first time I was going to be home in quite a while, and I really needed some closure at that point in my life.

The next week came around and my plane had landed in the 20 Cedar St area. My childhood best friend picked me up at the airport and took me to his home, where I anxiously waited for the next day's meeting.

I arrived at the office of the cold case unit the very next morning. I walked inside and checked in with the receptionist. I was then escorted inside a large conference room and sat down with the detectives. I asked them about the intricate parts of the crime that I didn't know, but they wouldn't tell me much about the case, due to the fact it was still an active investigation. They did let me in on the fact that they had looked into multiple suspects with most leads ending up going nowhere. The investigators told me that it was a very difficult case to solve, because most of the suspects and witnesses from the case were drug addicts. As years went on, the remainder of the suspects and witnesses had already died from living very unhealthy lifestyles.

I let the investigators know that I had a theory of my own and told them that I believed my uncle Vincent killed my mother. Once I was finished talking, the investigator told me that my uncle Vincent had been interviewed once before and there were no facts that lead anyone to believe he was the killer. I could never figure out why nobody thought there was even a slight chance that my uncle Vincent could've killed his own sister. I then thought back to when I read the newspaper articles from years ago when I found out that my mother was murdered. I thought about the section where my grandfather wrote that he believed he knew who killed my mother, and sent the police to interrogate that certain individual who lived in the same town as the methadone clinic. A suspect from the methadone clinic area was then questioned and actually admitted to being with my mother after she left the methadone clinic. I believe that the suspect who was interviewed was the individual that my grandfather had pointed finger at, but the detectives would never release that information to me. The investigation revealed that the suspect spent a short moment with my mother and quickly dropped her off at an undisclosed location down the street. The suspect then had a legitimate alibi to his whereabouts following and was no longer a suspect in my mother's murder. Since my mother was with someone after the methadone clinic, the detectives were also able to clear my uncle Vincent and wash his hands of any and all wrongdoing.

My uncle left with his sister one morning to the methadone clinic, twenty-five miles from 20 Cedar St and didn't return with her. I believe he really should've been a person of more importance. Bottom line, the meeting didn't have any information that really jumped out at me and I walked away with no answers to what really happened the day my mother was murdered.

A few days later, I boarded the airplane and was

headed back home to be with my wife and kids. When I arrived, my wife asked me how the meeting went. I told her that I received plenty of new information, but nothing gave me any clear answers. I told her that I felt a lot better about the situation, just knowing that I received what I believed was the undisputed truth about the case. I definitely wished that I would've been able to better understand what had happened though. I was able to ease that part of my life for a while, putting it to the side, and began to focus more on my wife and kids.

With a clearer mind, I again determined that having my new family was the best thing that ever happened to me. It allowed me to have the greatest and most permanent responsibility for all of my actions, and I wasn't going to make criminal-like choices anymore. I was happy as could be and loved my family as much as anyone could love. I had everything that I wanted, but begun to think about my brother Tony and Vincent Jr again, who didn't have the same luck as I did. I hadn't spoken to either of them in quite a few years during the time I was in my bad personal decision recovery stage. I was feeling good, my mindset was right, and I wanted to find them and reach out. I wanted more than anything to have my 20 Cedar St family back, and saw it necessary to get them on the same track as me. I wanted to tell them about how I was finally doing the right thing all the time, and how good it felt deep down inside.

I didn't have their phone numbers and that was the way they liked it, the less people who knew their whereabouts, the better. I always considered the two of them true loners, just like I had once been. It was extremely difficult to find or contact either one of them, so I contacted as many people as I knew around the 20 Cedar St area.

Almost everyone I had spoken to said they hadn't seen either one of them in years. Some said that Tony was probably back in prison, which was his normal routine. An old friend of mine said he saw Vincent Jr about three or four years earlier at a large Casino about one-hundred miles from 20 Cedar St, and was asked by my cousin to borrow fifteen-hundred dollars. This old friend told me that my cousin had been released from prison a year or so earlier for assault. A few others told me that he still had a bad gambling, beer, and aggression problem.

With somewhere to start, I vowed to locate my 20 Cedar St brothers again. I always considered Vincent Jr my brother, and he considered me to be the same. I had decided to call multiple state prisons in the 20 Cedar St area. After a few weeks of searching, I had finally located Tony. He was locked up in state prison again, for what I think was at least his fourth prison sentence. He was doing time for possession with intent to distribute, but was set to be released within a year or so. I started to keep in touch with him, but right away he wanted me to start sending him money to his prison account. He told me about how bad the food was in prison and that he didn't have money for soap or anything. I told him not to lie to his brother and to stay away from the drugs and off the prison poker tables. I told him that I wouldn't be sending him any money, but would agree to put a few dollars on his phone account so we could keep in touch outside from our letters. I explained to him that he needed to eat the three meals a day provided and to serve his prison time like a man. He didn't agree with my mentality, but at least my brother Tony and I were finally back in contact. It was too bad that we still hadn't seen one another since the days when we lived together at 20 Cedar St. I desperately wanted to find my cousin and decided to put a large amount of effort into locating him.

Chapter 12

It was early fall and I began the manhunt for Vincent Jr. I hadn't spoken to him in years and his birthday had just passed. The first thing I wanted to do when I contacted him was to wish him a happy birthday for the first time in many years. I began my search by calling multiple police stations and prisons within a two-hundred square mile radius of 20 Cedar St, but had no luck finding him. I called around for nearly two months before I almost gave up, but decided to begin searching archived newspaper articles during my free time at work.

After searching for my cousin through numerous archived newspapers, I came up with about five hits for my cousin Vincent Jr. I read the first article that caught my eye, but I didn't think much of it because of the nature of the article, but decided to read it anyway. The article contained his name, but his age was too young to be Vincent Jr. I opened up a couple of the other hits and got similar articles about a Vincent Jr, but his age was still too young. I decided that I needed to read the articles since I had no other information leading me to his whereabouts. Sitting at my work desk, I deciphered through the article until my mind finally allowed me to accept what I was reading. I began to cry at work while staring at a computer screen, similar to my crying episodes from a few years earlier. I finally understood why my cousin's age didn't match up. The article that I had been reading was from more than two years earlier. It was hard to believe that not a single person knew about the incident, it only happened one-hundred miles away from 20 Cedar St.

The next morning, I got myself together and called the local town police department where the incident had occurred. When I called, I was hoping that what I read wasn't true. The phone rang and it was answered by a very polite officer. I stated that I was Vincent Jr's brother and was calling to confirm if what I read in an almost three-year-old newspaper article was true. The officer was blown away by the fact that I called and he immediately put me in touch with the sergeant in charge. After speaking to the sergeant, I could tell that he still didn't believe who I was, so I stated that I wasn't Vincent Jr's biological brother, but was his first cousin and the closest related person to him. I then explained that even though we were first cousins, we were brothers and lived together for many years. The sergeant believed my story and told me everything he knew about what happened and verified that it was Vincent Jr that I was reading about in the old newspaper article.

Ten years earlier when I had sent my cousin packing from my apartment, in an effort to keep myself from getting into trouble with the military, I discovered that he moved about one-hundred miles away from 20 Cedar St. He continued working in the manual labor field and lived close to the casinos to fulfill his gambling habit. He had lived there for quite some time, only getting into documented trouble with the law on a couple occasions. He had kicked the crap out of some people, one to include a roommate. Vincent Jr seemed to otherwise have his mind straight from what I know, but he still couldn't kick the beer drinking, gambling habit, or childhood PTSD. I spoke to a previous girlfriend of my cousins from a few years before the incident had occurred, and she said, "He loved and always talked about his family." She told me that he was very caring and kind to her daughter, but struggled with emotional issues very badly. All the beer drinking, his bad temper, gambling, and uncontrollable crying at times, was enough for his girlfriend to send him packing as well. My cousin moved on from that relationship and his story was just starting from there.

I then understood that what I had read was true, and I needed to figure out what really happened on the day of that nearly three-year-old newspaper article. I needed to know what was going on in his brain to bring him to that type of behavior. The local law enforcement officers didn't have any more information for me about the case because it was still an ongoing investigation. They were able to give me the name of the hospital that Vincent Jr stayed at years earlier, so I contacted them. The hospital told me that the only person who visited him in his hospital bed was a young lady who was said to be his girlfriend.

I decided to get back with the incidents local law enforcement to ask them if they had any contact with anyone from our family. They told me that they did, and that the individual they spoke to and eventually met in person at the police station, was by far the "Coldest son of a gun" they ever met in their lives. Apparently, my uncle Vincent had been released from state prison a few years earlier from the past savage beating of his wife.

At the time of the incident, the police department was working with the hospital in an effort to contact my uncle Vincent, in order to get direction on life support concerns for my cousin. A few days after the incident had occurred, the police department finally got a hold of my uncle and told him what had happened. They explained to him that his son was currently at the hospital and on life support. My uncle Vincent stated to the police, "I don't have a son, and if you bother me again, I'll sue you." The police department tried one more tactic, stating to my uncle that Vincent Jr had cash money in his wallet. My piece of crap uncle made the one-hundred-mile trip to the police department once he heard that there was an opportunity to put some money into his own pocket.

Once my uncle arrived to the police station, he spoke to the sergeant in charge and demanded his son's wallet. The sergeant told him that he would have to properly identify himself as Vincent Jr's father. My uncle Vincent showed proper identification and answered a few questions, proving to be my cousin's father, and demanded again to see the wallet. The sergeant gave him the wallet and my uncle Vincent removed the hundreds of dollars that were in it, put the money in his pocket and said, "Don't you ever bother me again or I'll sue you." My uncle Vincent didn't even want to know about what happened to his son and didn't care, he just wanted the remaining cash that was in his wallet. The police department then asked if he would give the hospital guidance of keeping his son on or off life support. My uncle stated again, "I don't have a son, and if you bother me again, I'll sue you." The police department then notified the hospital and told them that they made contact with my uncle Vincent and provided them with his telephone number.

I was told this story from the police department and it didn't surprise me one bit about the evilness of my uncle. I then asked the police department for any other phone numbers that could help me figure out what was going on. The police department gave me the number to the State attorney's office who was handling the case and I contacted them immediately. The state attorney's office had very nice people working there, and after I verified that I was a caring relative of my cousin, they opened up to me. They gave me all the information I was looking for and the allowable facts of the ongoing case.

Six months prior to the incident taking place, my cousin met a younger attractive female named Claire. She seemed to be looking for someone to supply her with drugs and keep her high while her boyfriend was locked up in state prison. Vincent Jr only smoked pot and hated the sight of hard drugs after having to watch his junkie parents snort, swallow, and shoot all those years. My cousin had an idea and it soon became a reality. He liked nothing more in the world than beer drinking, gambling, and fist fighting, so he figured out a way to do at least two of them. He decided to rent out a hotel room on the weekends at his favorite casino and stationed Claire in the bedroom. He would get heroin for her addiction, keep her nice and high, and she agreed to stay in the hotel room for part of the weekend. He told her that if she wanted to be able to stay high, they would need to earn money in order to purchase the heroin. Claire did whatever it took to ensure she stayed high. Vincent Jr had his weekend dream right in front of him. He was able to stay at the poker table, drink beers all day long, and make easy money on the side. He was in the making of his one-woman casino prostitution business. He became known as the guy who had a prostitute in the casino hotel room, and she was good looking. I would guess that people would approach him at the poker table and pay him the standard fee for his services.

He would then send men to the room and notify his girlfriend on what was paid for.

Vincent Jr had money coming in while he was gambling and loved it, but a new problem arose. Claire's boyfriend was getting out from prison in just a few weeks and was very unhappy about what my cousin was doing with his girlfriend. Vincent Jr wasn't afraid of the man, and actually tried to schedule a good fist fight with him when he got out of prison. While incarcerated, Claire's boyfriend would call her from the inmate telephone account or from the cell phone that she smuggled into him. At times, my cousin would answer her cell phone and speak directly to the incarcerated boyfriend over the phone. The convict was extremely ticked off at Vincent Jr and told him that when he got out of prison in a few weeks, he was going to kill him. Vincent Jr told him that they didn't need to argue about the issue, instead they should make the situation work. My cousin said, "You can keep your girlfriend Monday through Friday, but I need her on the weekends for the casino," and then laughed. Vincent Jr told him that there was nothing wrong with sharing her. The convict was so upset, but was still incarcerated and unable to act.

A few weeks later had come around, and Vincent Jr heard that Claire's boyfriend had just been released from prison that day. Vincent Jr knew that the boyfriend was going to try to pick her up and take her away from the new lifestyle she'd been living, but he wasn't going to allow that. Vincent Jr left work early that day, went to Claire's house and waited for the boyfriend to show up. Claire told my cousin to leave or she would call the police. She told him that she used him and didn't need to prostitute anymore, because her boyfriend was going to feed her habit with clean money again. That absolutely ticked of my cousin more than anything. It wasn't about the prostitution money or even the fact that Claire was leaving him. My cousin felt as if he had been taken advantage of and didn't like the feeling. The new issue was about the principle of some guy thinking he was going to push aside Vincent Jr. Even though my cousin was doing something completely wrong and illegal, he had become very upset that he was made out to be the bad guy for only doing what was mutually agreed upon between Claire and himself.

Vincent Jr drove away from Claire's house to avoid the police, but waited right down the street, keeping a close eye on the home. Shortly after and just a few hours fresh out of prison, Claire's boyfriend pulled up to her house in his pickup truck. Vincent Jr approached the home a minute later with the intensions of laying a decent beating on Claire's boyfriend. Once my cousin parked his truck in front of the house, he was seen by the two of them. Claire's boyfriend quickly got into his own truck and she jumped him into the passenger seat. Claire's boyfriend took off quickly, but Vincent Jr

137

jumped into his own truck and began to follow from behind.

Soon enough, the minor tailgating by my cousin eventually turned into a ten-mile-high speed chase. Vincent Jr called Claire's cell phone and told her that if she got out of the truck he would agree to stop following, but she wouldn't. Claire's boyfriend was soon terrified of my cousin's size, shear anger, and the violence he portrayed. Claire and her boyfriend refused to call the police and decided to handle the situation by themselves.

Eventually, Vincent Jr was able to get Claire's boyfriend to lose control of his truck, slamming its side into a telephone pole, but the truck was still going. Miles later, my cousin was finally able to pass the truck and get in front of them at the town's main street intersection. Vincent Jr was able to block off two thirds of the road with his own truck, as he parked it sideways in the road. Vincent Jr jumped out of his truck and stood in the remaining part of the roadway. Claire and her boyfriend had come to a stop just shy of the intersection, then backed up a distance. Vincent Jr waived his hands up in the air and yelled "*Come on,*" wanting Claire's boyfriend to pull up beside and commence in the good fist fight he had been waiting for. It was too bad for my cousin though, because the freshly released convict who spoke so tough over the phone wasn't much of a tough guy, just someone who didn't pay his taxes.

Claire told her boyfriend to turn around, but instead he screamed, "*Forget him*," and floored his vehicle straight for Vincent Jr. Since my cousin was no murderer, just someone with childhood PTSD and an anger problem, he didn't expect what was next. The man didn't swerve out of the way, slow down, stop, or call the police. He continued to accelerate and drove right through Vincent Jr, launching him into the windshield. Claire's boyfriend continued to accelerate and intentionally swerved back and forth until Vincent Jr's body was thrown off at a high speed. Besides the injuries sustained from the initial impact, the major trauma was when my cousin's head slammed the concrete. Claire's boyfriend sped off and went to find somewhere to hide his truck. There were a few bystanders at the intersection and they were able to give vital information about the final moments of the incident to the police.

When the paramedics arrived to the scene, Vincent Jr was on the pavement making a grunting sound, indicative to someone with severe brain trauma. He was rushed to the hospital and immediately hooked up to life support. He was such a loner that nobody from the 20 Cedar St area ever knew where he was living. The hospital needed to find Vincent Jr's next of kin in order to see if his family would like to keep him hooked up to life support with the hopes of a recovery.

After a few days at the hospital, Vincent Jr was

still hooked up to life support. With help from the police department, the hospital was finally able to get into contact with my cousin's father, "Uncle Vincent." My uncle must've told the hospital the same thing as he told the police department, "I don't have a son, and if you contact me again I will sue you." I don't know what was actually said that day between my uncle and the hospital, but I do know that my uncle hated his son and his son hated him. Whichever tactic the hospital used to coerce my uncle into giving guidance on life support concerns, I will never know. My uncle finally had his chance to kill his son, and I believe it was his full intention to pull the plug that day, no matter the diagnosis of Vincent Jr.

I understand that it is difficult to believe that my uncle Vincent used that opportunity to try to finish off Vincent Jr, but if you grew up at 20 Cedar St, it would be easy to believe. I don't know what medical information was discussed between the hospital and my uncle that day over the phone, or if he had brain activity or not, but I still believe that the hospital should've done more to locate someone who cared. I'm sure that the phone call was a bit unethical, even without me knowing what was actually said. I truly don't believe that the hospital notified a next of kin that day, "They notified a murderer." The hospital met the bare minimum of the law and were able to annotate that particular phone call as receiving guidance on life support concerns by the next of kin. I'm very sure that it took a whole lot of persuasion to get my uncle to pull the plug on his son that he hated from the time he was born. Since there wasn't a single caring family member notified about my cousin's injuries, nobody actually received the medical diagnosis of Vincent Jr's injuries. There wasn't any real family at the hospital that day to properly assess the situation and stop their hands from pulling the plug if deemed necessary. The hospital did the bare minimum of trying to notify a caring family member and decided that after six days they would no longer keep my cousin alive. I don't know how the hospital could consider my uncle Vincent as proper notification of next of kin and consent to pull the plug if he didn't care about his son. Once the plug was pulled on Vincent Jr's sixth day in the hospital, he was dead at a very young age.

Despite what had happened between my cousin and Claire's boyfriend, I consider the hospital administrators negligent and my uncle Vincent as an accessory to the murder if my belief is correct. No matter what story the hospital could possibly tell me about their conversation over the phone with my uncle that day, I would never believe it unless it was pure evil.

My cousin was not the most decent person on the universe and so much more of the blame is on him. He was a grown adult and should've controlled his own criminal and ridiculous behavior. I do respect the fact that Claire cooperated with the police and snitched out her non-tax paying boyfriend, but that personal act of kind snitching was simply just survival mode to me. That's my opinion, but I could be wrong.

After hearing part of the story from law enforcement and reading its entirety on the formal pre-sentence investigation paperwork, I asked where the non-tax paying boyfriend was as that moment. After Claire's boyfriend slammed into my cousin and then launched him from the windshield, he hid his damaged truck at his brother's body shop. Luckily, an eye witness at the scene saw the name of the construction company on the side of the truck that struck my cousin. With that piece of information and the additional information Claire was able to give, the police issued an arrest warrant. The police later picked up Claire's boyfriend and put him in county jail to await trial. It had been almost three years from the time of the incident and the trial had not even begun to take place.

As time went by, there was still one more piece of information that nobody had yet to tell me, and the district attorney said to contact the local police department about it. I called back to the local police department and asked them where my cousin's body was buried. They then gave me the name and number to a funeral home. I called and spoke to a very polite employee at the funeral home and asked where my cousin was buried, because I wanted to

move him home to our family's 20 Cedar St cemetery plot. The director didn't answer my question
right away and was upset about something. I asked
if everything was alright and then he began to tell
me about the time he contacted my uncle Vincent,
asking him if he would come and identify his son's
body. My uncle Vincent said the same thing to him
as he said to the police department and probably the
hospital too, "I don't have a son, and if you contact
me again I'll sue you." Vincent Jr was forced by
law to stay frozen in a mortuary for over two years
because his evil father refused to identify his body.
My uncle Vincent was allowed to make life support
decisions for his son, but wouldn't identify his body
in order for him to be properly buried. I was enraged
about everything and wanted the opportunity to find
my uncle Vincent and punch the life out of his body.
I wasn't a scared kid anymore and I was determined
to find him in the near future.

With permission from the state and after years of
remaining frozen, Vincent Jr had eventually been
cremated and buried just a few months before I
found out about his death. The state had eventually
buried him in a numerical unmarked grave. The
fact that Vincent Jr's dad was such an evil person
had allowed for nobody to ever know that he was
dead or frozen for all those years, until I searched
for him and discovered it. I immediately contacted
the cemetery where he was buried and identified
who I was to their administrators through documen-

143

tation. I contacted just a few of Vincent Jr's best friends from the 20 Cedar St area where we all grew up and they were very saddened by the news. The cemetery dug up the cremations and I asked my cousins childhood best friend if he could make the drive to pick them up. I then contacted the local 20 Cedar St cemetery that contained the family head-stone and all six burial plots that my grandfather had purchased sixty years prior. I scheduled for my cousin to be buried within a week of his remains arriving home. I purchased a matching granite foot-stone in order to bury Vincent Jr with our family and the church was paid for their burial services. Vincent Jr was home and I felt like I had done the least I could do.

It was almost as if the curse of 20 Cedar St destined my grandfather to purchase six burial plots many years ago. The burial site contained my great-grandfather, grandfather, grandmother, mother, and Vincent Jr. There was only one cursed plot remaining and I wondered who it was meant for?

Four years after the murder of my cousin, the trial finally began. It only took a couple weeks to charge Claire's boyfriend with manslaughter and he was sentenced to fifteen years in state prison. The judge told him that he did not compare the case or my cousin's killer to, "Richard Gere in pretty woman." He then stated that after he screamed "Forget him" and ran through Vincent Jr, he took everything away from my cousin.

I had tried to collect any sentimental property of my cousins, but realized that whatever he had was already taken, similar to the property from 20 Cedar St when I was younger. I had also called around the local area where he was living, triple verifying to see if Vincent Jr had any children. I was not going to let the curse get a hold of another 20 Cedar St life, and was willing to take on any children my cousin may have fathered. I later found out that he didn't have any children. I learned a lot from all my calling around to the location where he'd been living. I discovered that he was disliked by many and his very few possessions to include his pickup truck were taken by unknown persons.

Since the day Vincent Jr was born, the curse of 20 Cedar St never gave him a chance of finding happiness or love in life. He was even hated by his own cursed and evil father.

Chapter 13

Time went on, and it was about six months after my son had been born. With so much going on in my head the previous year, I seemed to have missed the later term of my wife's pregnancy and the beginning stages of my son's life. Even though I understood what I was missing, I couldn't stop thinking about what happened to Vincent Jr.

I felt that it was time to get back on the phone and was determined to locate my uncle Vincent in order to make things right. There was only one problem at that time, the phone number I had received in the past was no longer a working number. It had been more than three years since the death of my cousin and I had to start from scratch in an effort to locate his evil father.

Soon enough, my older sister would be getting married and I booked a family vacation back to the 20 Cedar St area. My wife had never been to that part of the country and she was very excited. It was a nine-day trip and I set one day aside to ensure that I saw my brother Tony, but was extremely disappointed that I wasn't able to locate my uncle Vincent yet.

I had plenty of commitments while vacationing with my new family around 20 Cedar St. Visiting my brother Tony and attending my older sister's wedding were at the top of my list. My brother wasn't doing well and had just been released from prison again. I wanted to help him out as much as possible and I didn't want to lose my last brother. Tony had so many misdemeanor charges under his belt, had numerous felony convictions, but even more so, he was a drug addict. I hadn't seen him since I was about eighteen years old and it was well over a decade since then. I contacted him weeks before the trip to let him know I would be in the area.

After about five days on the family vacation, I let my brother know that I would take the hour and a half long drive to see him on the last day of our trip.

The day had arrived and I was finally going to see my brother Tony. He wanted to meet up with me at a fast food restaurant, which was right across the street from the halfway house he was living at. When my brother walked through the front glass doors of the fast food chain, we locked eyes. I felt like crying when I saw him, and it wasn't because I was sentimental. We gave each other a big hug, and all I could feel through his handed down and over-sized goodwill clothes was a very thin and drug addicted body. My brother's teeth had turned a grayish color from all the years of doing drugs. His nose was permanently affixed, halfway to his cheek from the last time it was broken in the streets. He had a healing stab wound on his right hand from a week prior when another junkie on the street tried to steal the little money my brother had. Tony was

147

attacked with a knife and used his hand to stop the blade from hitting his chest. Besides the initial hello, my brothers first words to me were, "I heard you're a cop or something like that, what a three-sixty that is, *Holy Crap!*" I told my brother that indeed I was a law enforcement officer, and a very changed person.

My brother only knew the person I used to be and also from the stories he probably had heard. Tony couldn't believe the huge turn around I had made with my life. My brother was so messed up and I could see how nervous and ashamed of himself he was when we saw each other. I thought we were going to spend the day together starting from that moment, but he couldn't. My brother couldn't handle the situation and had to go shoot heroin into his arm right away.

Tony met up with me at a local state park about an hour later and we talked about nonsense. After hanging out for a while, I took him to eat. I will never forget that meal, ever. What I could see most of the time was just the white of his eyes. His eyes kept rolling into the back of his head and he kept falling asleep and nodding off into his food. My wife kept waking him up and getting his attention, but the heroin was in control of his bodily functions. He was far too messed up to even have a simple conversation at that point.

Tony eventually got up to get some more Chinese food from the buffet, and my five-year-old son asked if he could go to the serving area with my brother. Tony said, "Let him come, it will be nice." I let my son go with him and watched very closely for the first minute and noticed that everything was going fine, so I went back to eating my food. My brother arrived back to the table about one minute later and sat down. I asked Tony where my son was, and he said, "Who?" I ran around the restaurant looking for my little boy. I went into the men's and women's restrooms, to include barging into the chef's kitchen area. After not finding him, I ran outside and found him playing about one-hundred feet from the restaurant on a mechanical horse, which was in front of a local drug store. My brother really was a disaster, and at that moment I could fully understand his situation. After the meal, I took my brother to the same drug store and bought him whatever necessity products I could, to at least make his next two weeks on the streets a little easier.

I had thought that seeing my brother was going to be like the old days when we played Atari, then Nintendo, and eventually Sega Genesis together, but I was wrong. I thought we were going to listen to some Guns and Roses or Twisted Sister, then throw the football around for a while. After seeing Tony, I felt just as bad as I did when I found out that Vincent Jr had been killed. To me, Tony was already dead, or at least I almost wished he was. I would've rather found out that he was dead than to see him like that. I had to get back to town and get ready to fly out, so I got a phone number from Tony in order to reach him when I returned home.

The vacation was over and the next morning we flew home. It seemed as if the only memory from the entire vacation to remain in my head was my drug addicted brother. Two days later and two-thousand miles away, I had tried calling Tony. I couldn't get a hold of him and was afraid that something happened to him from all the stress he endured from the recent day that we'd seen each other. I called a few local jails and police stations and found out that the morning after I flew home, he was arrested for receiving stolen property. I found out that he wasn't much of a drug distributer anymore and had turned into more of a thief. He had been stealing from stores all around the country to support his heroin addiction. With his latest arrest, he only had to serve six months in a minimum security facility, so I kept in touch with him throughout his prison sentence. I wanted so badly to help my brother, I really did. I explained to my wife that getting him away from the cursed 20 Cedar St home and the streets he hung around could possibly save him. Even though Linda was terrified, she knew how much it meant to me and agreed. My brother also agreed to come out and stay with us when he was released from prison, in an effort to clean up his addiction and his future.

It wasn't even a week after my return from the

20 Cedar St area vacation, and I had so much on my mind. Vincent Jr was dead, my brother Tony might as well have been dead, I was unable to locate my uncle Vincent, and I couldn't let go of my mother's unsolved murder. I needed to stay busy and decided to go into the backyard to see if my pool needed a cleaning, and it did. I began cleaning the pool, and for whatever reason I started to stare at the spading fork that was left behind by the previous owner. I never had any use for it, but always left it hanging with my other outside yard tools. I continued to clean the pool and began to think about my mother's unsolved murder even more. I thought back to what I'd read about my mother on the day I discovered the newspaper article in my grand-mother's wooden trunk. I started to think about the day when Vincent Jr told me that his dad had killed my mother. I started to think about how cold of a person my uncle was to his own son after he was murdered, and how cold he was for beating his wife to a pulp. I thought back to when he sunk his teeth into my grandmother's arm for a couple dollars. I thought about the story my grandmother's sister told me when my uncle returned home without his sister. I thought about a lot.

I continued cleaning the pool and began brain-storming the investigators words from the cold case meeting I had attended about eight months earlier. I scanned my brain for any kind of answers until something of importance had finally jumped into my cranium that made sense to me. My brain finally put information together and I connected the dots. It must've been intelligence that I received from a higher being or just unanswered reasoning. I remembered when the investigators had mentioned some information about my mother's body being removed from the shallow grave by the local police officers. The detectives told me that her body had puncture wounds. The cold case investigators told me that the wounds were of no importance to the case and were most likely caused by the police officer's shovels poking her as they dug her from the ground.

I remembered something from that previous meeting very clearly, even though it was nearly eight months earlier. I had asked the investigator how wide the puncture wounds were, where they were located, a count of how many, and their dimensions. At the time I had asked those questions I had no idea where I was leading myself, but it's possible that someone else was asking the questions for me. The puncture wounds were stated to be non-life threatening, had nothing to do with the murder, and definitely happened after her death. The cause of death was still strangulation, but the measurement of punctures that were revealed by the investigators had jumped out at me as I was cleaning the pool and staring at my spading fork. The investigator had given me a count of how many puncture wounds were present on my mother's body, along with their isolated location. I was told the width of each puncture hole, with each having the same exact measurement. I was then told the distance between each of the punctures, revealing that they all had nearly the same measurements between them.

At the time of the cold case meeting, the measurements of the puncture wounds didn't have much meaning to me, but while cleaning my pool I found a direct resemblance between the measurements and the spading fork that I was staring at. I quickly put down my pool vacuum, ran inside the house and got the tape measure from my tool box. With a lot of anxiety, I measured the exact spading fork as the one which had hung on the 20 Cedar St garage wall. I discovered that the measurement of the spading fork was nearly exact to the measurement of the punctures revealed to me by the detectives. I believed that I had found a match.

I dropped my measuring tape and thought about the spading fork that I stabbed my sister in the foot with. I thought about how it was the only yard tool we owned at our cursed 20 Cedar St home.

I began to think about the police officers at the scene of my mother's murder. I thought about what the investigator had said about the police officers, that they were the ones who probably punctured the wounds into my mother's body while digging her up, and I said, "No way!" I remember reading the old newspaper article which stated that the police actually did arrive on scene with shovels to dig up my mother's body, so the possibility was there.

I did some investigating of my own and contacted as many people as I could with knowledge of my mother's case. I learned that spaded shovels did indeed arrive at the scene to dig up her body. It was also revealed to me that the first shovel had hit my mother's body, but it was the only one to do so. With the first shovel striking the dirt, the officers immediately discovered that my mother was right there, barely covered by peat moss and a very thin layer of loose soil. The shovels were immediately placed on the ground and she was removed by hand.

My mother's body had only been hit a single time, so how did she receive the other adjacent wounds? I don't believe my mother's body received even a single puncture wound that day, and she especially didn't receive multiple wounds from the one and only shovel that hit her.

The grave had been dug very narrow and extremely shallow. I thought to myself, "If I was burying someone that I killed, I would put them as deep into the ground as I possibly could, with the hopes that they'd never be found." I also realized that it would be nearly impossible to dig that deep with a spading fork.

My mother's belongings were annotated as being scattered across the ground near the shallow grave. It was later revealed to me that her belongings had never been scattered, just the items from her purse.

My mother's clothing was neatly folded and placed under a large bush, as if by someone who cared. Her remaining items were also neatly placed and situated in the same location.

Over the years, I've come up with my own reen-actment of what happened the day my mother was murdered. I've created her last day on this earth, based on theory. My mother's case is unsolved, but below is my most logical version of the events that possibly unfolded.

My mother and uncle Vincent left 20 Cedar St by vehicle one morning, heading to the methadone clinic to get their fix. After receiving their metha-done, they returned to my uncle's vehicle. On the drive home, my uncle began to argue with my mother, demanding her to give up some drugs and pocket cash. After she refused, he quickly lost his temper, pulling the car off the road. My uncle went for my mother's purse, but she wouldn't let go. He pulled her closer, then began to strangle her in the front seat of his car, until she was dead. Realizing what he did, my uncle quickly became nervous. He drove my mother's lifeless body back to 20 Cedar St, with the intensions of telling my grandfather. When my uncle arrived at 20 Cedar St, he noticed that my grandfather's vehicle wasn't there. He pulled his car into the garage for a quick moment to assess the situation. He continued to panic, glancing at the spading fork hanging on the wall. He came up with a quick plan, deciding to take my

155

mother's body to a secluded area down the road, similar to a lovers' lane. He grabbed the spading fork from the wall, placed it in his trunk, and reversed out from the garage. Once he arrived, he drove his vehicle down the secluded dirt road, knowing nobody would be there until nightfall. He parked his vehicle, then carried my mother's body into the heavily dense area. After placing her on the ground, he went back to the car for the spading fork and her belongings. He stripped her of her clothes, making it look like a sexual relationship gone wrong. He quickly dug the incredibly shallow and narrow grave using the worst tool imaginable, a spading fork. He picked up my mother's body and placed her in the grave. My uncle took hold of the spading fork, stood over my mother, then stabbed her, ensuring he wasn't burying his sister alive. He quickly packed a thin layer of soil and peat moss on top of her. My uncle grabbed her purse and dumped it out, looking for the drugs and money he was after in the first place. He then picked up my mother's clothes from the ground, checking the pockets for a hidden stash. As my uncle held his sisters clothing in his hands, he became sentimental. He folded her clothes, placing them under a large bush and out of the weather. My uncle picked up the spading fork, placed it in the trunk, and drove back to 20 Cedar St. After pulling into the garage, he immediately hung the spading fork on the wall and went inside to wash up. When *entering the house, he bumped into my grand-mother and aunt, bringing me to believe that the statement I had received years earlier from my aunt was completely true.*

My uncle was an incredibly intelligent man, and definitely had the brain capacity to setup an entire murder scene. He also changed moods and person-alities as often as most people change their under-wear. He seemed to be bi-polar and schizophrenic all in one, allowing for myself to understand how he could kill and care at the same time.

About a week after my mother's disappearance, her grave and belongings were eventually spotted in the woods by a local hunter. The murder was then made public, with the story making front page headlines. I believe that my uncle Vincent had become extremely nervous about the possibility of being caught and confessed the murder to my grandfather at that time. My grandfather would've been heartbroken, but knowing the amount of protection and love he gave to his children, he would've done whatever necessary to ensure his son didn't get caught.

I began to think about the old newspaper article which stated my grandfather had sent the police on a lead to question who he believed was possibly the killer. My grandfather sent the police to the methadone clinic area, which was the last known location where my uncle had been seen with my mother. I believe my grandfather created a person of interest to the police, in order to give my uncle an alibi. This individual would become the first known person to be with my mother after my uncle Vincent "Supposedly" left her at the methadone clinic to hang out with friends. I believe that my grandfather coerced that individual into lying to the police, allowing for my uncle Vincent to be removed as a suspect in the case. My grandfather loved his children no matter what, and would definitely coerce someone into lying, rather than lose both of his children forever. Without a doubt in my mind, I believe my uncle and mother left the methadone clinic together that day.

From what I know, there was one witness who claimed to have seen my mother alive at a bar and motel establishment the afternoon she went missing. This statement would seem very convincing to many, since this establishment was very close to where her body was found. I believe that my grandfather coerced another person into telling the police a phony statement, creating yet the final alibi for my uncle.

The cold case unit has traveled the world searching for my mother's killer with a number of misleading accusations. I believe that my theory is the most convincing out there.

My grandfather knew what he was doing when he put out the statement in the local newspaper asking to be contacted with any information leading to an arrest. With his mob connections, my grandfather could have easily forced anyone into saying anything, retracting what their eyes may have seen and their ears may have heard. I believe that my grandfather and the locals who were interviewed, had taken the local police on a wild goose chase.

The old rumor that had spread like wildfire in our 20 Cedar St town about my grandfather and his connected people finding the killer and having him wacked, all seemed like lies and decoys even more so. I think that the rumor of my grandfather's people finding and killing the suspect was intended for the locals to stop looking into the case so much. That rumor did have some truth to it, which made it seem all the better for my grandfather and my uncle Vincent. The rumored retaliation killing in which I just discussed is archived by people who track and follow all murders which occurred by a certain Italian crime family. It doesn't say why this individual was killed, but it says he was and how it was done. I believe that the rumor of this man being my mother's killer was strictly a diversion technique by my grandfather. I believe that my grandparents lost their only daughter in a horrendous way and didn't want anyone to find out who the true killer was. If so, they would lose their last child to prison for the remainder of his life.

I began to recall back to a time when I was about ten years old and remember walking up the stairs behind my older sister. I remember that day clearly, as I decided to slap my older sister on the butt. My older sister then yelled out, "*Grandpa, Jason slapped my butt.*" I thought nothing of what I did. I had done so many stupid things in my childhood and my grandfather had never once laid a hand on me. My grandfather had never even used a curse word in front of me and never acted in a way to make me even feel slightly uncomfortable. This occasion was very different though. My grandfather had blown a gasket because I had slapped my sister on the butt. Maybe he thought I used physical violence or committed a sexual act towards my sister, but I will never know. We were a brawling and mischievous home, and this butt slap was absolutely nothing in comparison to our normal behavior.

I can remember my brother Tony throwing a Rubik's cube at me as hard as he could and the corner of it hitting me in the forehead. The Rubik's cube penetrated my forehead and I had blood running down my face, but my grandfather never blinked. That is just one of many incidents that occurred at our 20 Cedar St home where my grandfather never reacted to our mischievous violence. This is why the butt slapping incident has a lot of meaning. Maybe my grandfather was reminiscing about what really happened thirty years ago, and saw me as my uncle Vincent and my older sister as my mother. Maybe my uncle would do inappropriate things to his sister when he was younger, which eventually spiraled out of control and resulted in murder. I truly have no idea and am simply speculating. Either way, my grandfather had blown a fuse and came running at me and yelled, "*Do you like touching your sister, do you?*" He did not say, do you like touching girls or women, he said, "Do you like touching your sister?" He then grabbed me by my penis and threw me on the floor. He put one foot on my chest and started to pull on my penis as if he was going to rip it off and yelled, "*Don't you ever touch your sister's butt again or I will rip your penis off!*"

I was so terrified and in shock, not because he almost ripped my penis off, but because my grandfather had never acted that way to any of us in our entire lives. I wonder now, was it the fact that my uncle Vincent did indeed kill his own sister and had done extremely inappropriate things to her at one point in their lives. Is that what led my grandfather to blow up on me like he did? Maybe it was just the fact that a brother put his hands on his sister and my grandfather flashbacked to the horrible secret that he was keeping from the world. I believe that my grandfather saw myself as my uncle and my sister as my mother, and saw the underlining problems which lead to the murder, believing that it was right in front of him all over again. Overall, I wasn't able to pinpoint what that penis tearing incident truly revealed, but I believe it meant something extremely significant between my mother and uncle

161

Vincent.

I eventually called the detectives and told them my complete theory and reasoning of why I believed my uncle Vincent was the murderer. They heard me, but they never listened. Nothing that I have discussed with law enforcement has ever mattered, because the investigators will never believe that my uncle Vincent was the killer. The cold case unit already made it very clear to me that my uncle Vincent was questioned once, and there was no hard evidence connecting him to the murder. I decided to continue putting in more hard work into finding who I believed was my mother's killer, "Uncle Vincent."

Chapter 14

My brother Tony was still in prison, but was soon to be released. I kept in touch with his case worker at the correctional facility and purchased him a bus ticket, a plane ticket, and sent him the nicest clothes and shoes I had in my closet. I wanted him to feel good about himself when he was traveling the long distance to my home. I couldn't believe that my brother was really going to try to change his life, and I was happy to be a part of helping him. The day had come and my brother was released from prison. The bus ticket was never used, the plane ticket went to waste, and the nearly five-hundred-dollar wardrobe that I sent him was probably sold to purchase drugs. I realized that my brother didn't want help, or maybe he felt like I did when I was a dirt-bag, only feeling comfortable around my own kind. I didn't question my brother about the situation and still tried my best to keep in touch with him. Luckily there was still one cursed burial plot remaining at the cemetery, and that's when I was able to confirm who it was meant for.

I continued searching for my uncle Vincent and was pulling clues to hopefully identify his location. I didn't have the money to pay a private investigator to locate my uncle and it had become very difficult for me to find free time to continue my search. I was always working and helping my wife with our kids as much as I could.

I was still determined to find him and wasn't going to give up the search for my evil uncle, even though I was two-thousand miles away. I realized that I never asked the funeral home that held my cousins body for a contact number when I began the search for my uncle Vincent. I guess that I decided not to ask them for a phone number since they told me they got my uncles number from the police department who had already given their only number to me. I decided to call the funeral home anyway and asked the funeral director if he could give me any old contact numbers that he still had for my uncle Vincent. He had given me a few numbers, with one being different than any number I had received in the past. I was surprised that they still had any information at all, not to mention a different number. I took the new number over the phone and thanked the man, but I didn't believe it would lead me anywhere since it was from years prior. I called the number with hopes that it would lead me to my evil uncle. Instead, it went straight to a landline answering machine, which stated the name of the woman who was living at the home. I hung up the phone realizing that it was probably just another old number, but decided to call once again. There was no answer the second time either, just the same old recording. I decided to leave a message, just in case my uncle was living at that location. I said, "Hello, I am looking for my uncle Vincent, this is his nephew Jason Salvino, I want to ask my uncle some questions about the murder of my mother and also why he neglected his son's death?" I then finished the message leaving my call back number. I had decided to call a few more times over the next week, and repeatedly left the same message without ever getting a response. I knew that one day I would eventually find my uncle and have my chance to come face to face with him.

About one full month had gone by since I had left those messages on that woman's landline, and I still hadn't heard anything back. Just at that moment, I got a phone call from the 20 Cedar St town police department, who told me that my uncle Vincent had just passed away. The police department had my number on file since I had a relative working there. The officer gave me the phone number to a police department about forty miles away from 20 Cedar St who was handling my uncle's case. I called the police department and verified some personal questions. The police department then felt comfortable talking to me and let me in on the case. It was pretty simple, my uncle died from a drug overdose about one month after I left those voice messages on an undetermined person's answering machine. I asked the police department if they had a contact number to reach the location where he was living, and the officer said that they did. That was when the officer gave me the identical phone number that I had recently left the voice messages on. They said it was the phone number to the house that my uncle and his girlfriend were living in.

A few days had gone by and I placed another call to the same number as a month earlier. The phone call was actually answered, and it was my late uncle's girlfriend. I didn't ask her about the reasons of why my uncle didn't return my calls, and I didn't ask if anyone even listened to the messages I had left, I didn't need to. I asked her to tell me about my uncles last years and what she knew of him. She spoke very highly of him and talked about how much of a character he was. She was right in one sense, he was very intelligent, a talented musician, and could tell crazy stories of his past to entertain crowds of people. I discovered that she didn't know about his violent and evil past. I then asked her about his drug overdose. She told me that he had been hooked on pills because of a past injury, and that's what caused the overdose. I asked her how he was injured and she told me the story. I guess my uncle and his girlfriend weren't paying their mortgage and the lender was in the process of foreclosing on their home. The mortgage company had enough of my uncle and wanted him out of their house more than anything. The mortgage company decided to break the law themselves and cut the power to the home when my uncle and his girlfriend were still residing there. The power was cut just as my uncle was making his way down the homes interior flight of stairs. With the lights suddenly cut off, he tumbled down the flight of stairs, injuring his neck and other parts of his evil body. I had heard enough from the nice woman and ended the call politely.

My uncle Vincent had been an extremely heavy drug user since his early twenties. After forty years of shooting up and swallowing drugs, I knew that it wasn't going to be an injury from a few years earlier to cause him to overdose from pills. He was the heavy weight champion of the world drug user, and I refuse to believe that he all of a sudden had a drug overdose from an injury a few years earlier. I know he heard the messages I left him and became nervous and ashamed of his secret. I think he believed that I was beginning to uncover the truth about my mother's death and was tracing his steps. I knew he would never want to go back to prison and spend the remainder of his life behind bars. He simply could've felt so disgusted in himself for what he had done to his sister many years earlier that he intentionally ended his life. My uncle could've heard around town that I was looking into him as the killer of my mother and that I also wanted to settle the score for what he did to his son. I'm sure he heard that I was coming for him and knew that I was going to make things right for my mother and Vincent Jr.

Nobody had ever asked my uncle Vincent questions about the murder of my mother or confronted him for what he had done to his son. I had become the first to do so after addressing him over the recorded answering machine. He may have heard my messages and began getting higher than ever to relax his guilty conscience, until one day shortly after when he intentionally or unintentionally lost his life.

I don't believe that anybody was supposed to know who the murderer of my mother was, except for my uncle Vincent and my grandparents. I believe my grandparents covered up the facts of the case for so many years, right up until the day they died. That is my speculation, but who am I to override the cold case unit who told me that my theory of my uncle had no truth to it. There are only three known people in this world to have ever said with their own mouths, that my uncle Vincent killed my mother, and I am the only one of them who is still alive.

I later found out that the girlfriend of my uncle Vincent was going to bury his cremations in the local cemetery of where he'd been living. Against my sibling's wishes, against my late uncle's girlfriend, and against Vincent Jr's close friends, I decided to override the burial. I wouldn't allow my evil uncle to be buried outside of the 20 Cedar St cemetery. My grandfather always wanted to be buried with his children and it was one of his wishes before he died. It was where our entire family was buried and where my grandfather and the curse had designated everyone to be. Many people were disgusted with my intensions of bringing my evil uncle home. Close friends of my cousin didn't want to see his evil father buried next to him. Everyone understood the way his father treated him from birth and all the way through his death. A few close friends of my cousin had told me that they weren't going to allow the priest to bury my uncle's remains next to Vincent Jr. Others didn't want my uncle buried with the rest of my family for the same reason, because of his pure evilness.

The curse of 20 Cedar St was so powerful that it kept affecting generation after generation. I needed to figure things out like an adult and not a child, so I started to think like a grown man. If my great-grandfather wasn't a violent bootlegger with connections, then maybe my grandfather wouldn't have become one of the gambling entrepreneurs of his era either. The chances are that, if my grandfather would've been a regular father who spent more time with his kids and less time doing illegal activity, then maybe his daughter wouldn't have been a murdered drug addict and his son not a violent drug addict. It's quite possible that if my mother wasn't a drug addict and would've spent quality time with her children instead of stealing and shooting up, then maybe some of her kids wouldn't have screwed up so much in life. It's possible that my brother Tony could've been a successful person instead of a drug addict and convicted felon. I would like to think that if my uncle Vincent hadn't been such a violent drug addict, that maybe my cousin wouldn't have served his own prison time for assault, or had a violent temper, an alcohol problem, and a gambling addiction. It's quite possible that my cousin would still be alive today and maybe wouldn't have been involved in stupid crap like prostituting that woman. If past generations of my family were more open to good honest work, better communication with their kids, and more family time, then the old saying that crap runs downhill, might not have become a cursed reality for 20 Cedar St. Many of us who grew up at 20 Cedar St were just doing what we were taught as children and from past generations.

After understanding what had been going on at 20 Cedar St for the last one-hundred years a little clearer, I didn't see any problem in burying my uncle Vincent with his family. There wasn't one man who was better than any other inside of 20 Cedar St, to include myself. I realized that none of us ever learned a darn thing from one another over the years. Even if I believe that my uncle murdered his own sister, even if believe he was an accomplice in the murder of his son for neglect, I still understood that he belonged at our family's burial site. After I explained the cursed 20 Cedar St snowball effect to family and Vincent Jr's close friends, they started to understand. It wasn't just the case of my uncle Vincent being an evil individual, but a century long curse and a lack of parenting and guidance over four generations. Even though nobody had a problem with the burial anymore, they still refused to have any part of it.

If there is such a thing as the afterlife, everyone from 20 Cedar St would finally have their chance to mend what they had done to each other over the past one-hundred years. All of my deceased family members would have eternity to build new relationships and correct their past family problems. Either way, my grandfather purchased six cursed burial plots and the final plot was now going to be filled by my uncle Vincent. I thought to myself, "Thank god, my brother Tony is going to be alright." There were no more burial plots left and I saw a decent future awaiting my brother.

I telephoned to the funeral home which had the cremations of my uncle Vincent shortly after. I had to send them documentation proving that I was next of kin, and had some minor legal paperwork filed in order to override his girlfriend's right to the cremated remains. I asked my older sister who was still living in the area if she would take the forty-five-minute drive to pick up our uncles remains. I also asked her if she could keep the cremated remains at her house until the burial. My older sister quickly refused and stated that she wanted nothing to do with burying him with the rest of our family, or just burying him in general. Months went by and my uncle's remains were still at the funeral home. It was similar to, but not even close to the two years his son was forced to remain frozen. I was two-thousand miles away and there wasn't much I could do about it. Nobody would pick up his cursed remains and the burial was set up and paid for. After a few days had gone by, I had to cancel the burial and figure out a way to get the whole problem taken care of. The funeral home really started to bug me about my uncle's cremated remains, and were about to start charging me for storing his cremations.

I spoke with the funeral home the following day and asked them if they could drop off the remains at my older sister's house, which was about a forty-five-minute car ride away. I told them to bring the cremations to that location if they wanted my late uncle off their hands. I never told my older sister that the cremations were going to her house and tried to catch her off guard, knowing she'd have a major problem with it. The funeral home actually agreed to drive the cremations to my sister's home, just because they wanted nothing to do with the problem anymore.

The following day, the remains of my uncle Vincent arrived at my older sister's home. The doorbell was rung and an employee of the funeral home presented the cremations to my sister. She quickly refused to accept the urn and the employee became upset, but kept it professional. The funeral home just didn't know what to do with the cremations any longer. My sister finally told the employee to place the urn on the front lawn or anywhere outside of the home, not wanting to let her uncle Vincent into her home dead or live. I received a call from my older sister telling me that the urn was outside her home and she was going to leave it there. I thought she would soften up over time, but she didn't. The urn sat outside in the weather and I realized that we still had different views on the situation. I called my best friend from the 20 Cedar St area and asked him if he could drive to my sister's home and retrieve my uncle Vincent's remains. He then wanted to know where he was supposed to bring the cremated remains. I asked him if he could keep the urn at his house for a few days until I could re-schedule a burial. He said he had no problem picking it up, but nobody at his house wanted my uncle's evilness in their presence either. Out of respect, they agreed to keep the urn in their home for a couple nights. I asked my best friend to drive to my sister's home to pick up the remains that Saturday morning in preparation for the Monday burial. Just as my best friend was leaving for the urn, my older sister called him and said, "Don't waste the trip, I'm heading that way and I'll drop it off at your house." I don't think she was willing to take the chance of someone not showing up, so she took the urn herself, making sure that what was left of Uncle Vincent was nowhere near her home. My best friend received the urn and kept it at his home for a couple nights. He said that it was a few of the very creepiest nights ever, just knowing that my crazy uncle Vincent was in his house.

The burial took place on a Monday morning and not a single person attended, with the worst thing ever happening next. I called the local church to thank them for the burial and they were happy to inform me that they saved an extra burial plot by only digging and burying my uncle Vincent in a half plot. The church told me that they re-structured their paperwork and that the burial site still held one more cremation plot. I told the church that I didn't ask for them to bury my uncle in a half plot. I believed they were going to bury his cremations in a full plot, just like they'd done with Vincent Jr. The church told me that they did it just in case there was someone else in the future who needed to be buried at the 20 Cedar St gravesite. I immediately knew who they were talking about, my brother Tony. I had questioned the validity of the curse once before, but realized again that the curse was for real, and this was definitely a sign of its strength.

The earlier decision to bury all of my family together at the 20 Cedar St burial site was the right thing to do and what my grandfather had always wanted. Once deceased, the curse would lift and my 20 Cedar St family would finally have the chance to make amends with one another.

Chapter 15

I realized that I had been away from 20 Cedar St for so long, and believed that I was part of the cause of everything that had gone wrong over the past decade. I strongly felt that if I'd been back home, I could've stopped Vincent Jr from behaving the way he did, and he would still be alive today. I felt as if I could've straightened out my brother Tony if I was there. I even believed that if I moved my family back to the 20 Cedar St area earlier, I could've received a murder confession from my uncle Vincent before he overdosed and died. I even wanted to move back to the 20 Cedar St area to show everyone how well my life finally turned out. I wanted to show off my wife and kids, and to let everyone see that I turned out to be a decent human being.

I told my wife that we needed to move back to the 20 Cedar St area if I was going to be truly happy. She then said to me, "Why do you need that place to make you happy, your family is right here." I was still unsure of who my family actually was. I thought to myself, "Is my family 20 Cedar St, or is it my wife and kids?" I explained to her that my past was being erased and I wanted to have some of it left. I told her that I wanted to be able to drive to my older sister's house to visit her whenever I felt the need. I also wanted the opportunity to have a few cups of coffee with my brother Tony before he overdoses or gets killed in the streets. She somewhat understood about what I was saying, but still disagreed. Linda loved me so much that she actually agreed to move to the 20 Cedar St area, just to make me happy.

I had begun to apply for jobs within a fifty-mile radius of 20 Cedar St. The competition was tough, especially since I was applying for management positions in my law enforcement field, and living so far away didn't help.

As time went by, my wife became pregnant again and we were soon to be having our fourth child, a boy. She started to get a little weary about moving with a baby in her belly, but I was still determined. I continued applying for law enforcement work near 20 Cedar St because I was truly looking to be there for the rest of my life.

As time went on, I hadn't heard anything back from any positions. Before I knew it, my wife gave birth to our baby boy. I was very happy and proud to have another child, and being lonely for so many years, I seemed to have been creating a household that would never allow me to be alone again. I said to myself, "Maybe my wife is right, maybe my family is right here." Right or wrong, I still wanted to go back to the 20 Cedar St area to repair what was left of my childhood family.

I had so much going on in my head at that time and didn't know what to think anymore. There were so many unanswered questions filling my brain that I couldn't think straight. I woke up one morning with an idea that would possibly clear my mind. I decided to begin writing a book. I hoped that it would help clear my mind and possibly make sense to all my unanswered thoughts and questions about my life. I never imagined that I would learn so much about myself from writing.

While typing away, I thought about a lot. I even thought about how bad everything turned out to be for my brother Tony. I knew that I still wanted to help him and tried to contact him by phone. Luckily, I was able to get into contact with him and immediately realized that he was doing no better than before. We talked about a lot and I told him that I was writing a book. He asked me where I was trying to go with the book and what goal I was trying to accomplish. I talked to him about how we both found out in different ways of how our mother died. I told him about how our family never talked to one another about our problems. I explained to him that we were never told the truth about so much, for what was believed by others to be for our own good. I told him that I wanted to write about the cursed 20 Cedar St home and about some of the stories that took place inside of it. I then asked him if it was alright to include the story of how his father Douglas had died. He said, "That's fine, but why would anyone care about some guy dying from a brain aneurism?" I didn't know what to say to my

177

heroin addicted brother at that instance. Tony was almost forty years old and still didn't know how his father had died. I had no idea he didn't know, just like my brother and cousin had no idea that I didn't know about how my mother had died. This again was living proof that my 20 Cedar St family never talked about anything. Tony was still believing the story that our grandmother told us so many years ago. I would've still believed my grandmothers story just the same, especially if I hadn't questioned and investigated my own life so much as I got older. I very cautiously told my brother that the story our grandmother told us about his father dying was just another tale, similar to the barbeque story of our mother's death.

I began to tell him the story as he was waiting at a bus stop, talking to me on his prepaid phone. I told my brother Tony the true story like this. "Tony, way back when you were only about six months old, Grandma and Grandpa took our mother and yourself on a vacation to the cottage, but your dad decided to stay back. A couple days later, your dad called our mother and said, 'Hurry back home, I have a bunch of drugs for us.' Our mother told your dad that she couldn't come home for a few more days, because grandpa drove and she was without a car. The next day, nobody was able to get a hold of your father, so our mother sent some friends to look for him. The very next afternoon, grandpa received a phone call from the 20 Cedar St area police department explaining to him what had happened. The police chief told grandpa that it wasn't proven yet, but highly likely that your dad and two of his friends had robbed a local pharmacy and stole a bunch of pills. Despite the police department's leads, there were many reasons why your father was suspected of the crime. The main reason was that the police found a bunch of pills in your dad's bedroom that matched what was robbed from the pharmacy. The other reason was that your father's dead body was also in the room. He had died from a drug overdose."

My brother Tony took a long pause and then asked me how sure I was about the story, and I told him that it wasn't a story, it was the facts. He asked me a second time, and I told him loudly, *"Really Tony, that's what happened."* Those were nearly the exact same words that my cousin said to me when I didn't believe him about the statement he made about his dad killing my mom. I then said to him, "I wish Grandma never told us those tales." I made it known to my brother that our grandmother was trying to do right, but as we could see right then and there, it only made things worse. My brother replied with, "I always thought my father was a clean guy, at least that's what Grandma always told me." He then said, "Not that I wouldn't have been all messed up like I am, but maybe if I'd known that my father was a robbing, overdosing drug addict, it possibly could've scared me away from the drugs when I was younger, now look at me." My brother took another long pause and said, "Hey Jason, my bus is here, I have to go, I'll call you later."

Time went by following the conversation I had with my brother, and I continued applying for jobs in the 20 Cedar St area. So much time had passed that my wife had given birth to our fourth child. As I continued to find a way back to 20 Cedar St, even so much more time had passed. Before I knew it, my wife was pregnant again and our fifth child was on the way. I continued applying for law enforcement jobs for so long that my wife eventually gave birth to our fifth child, a girl. We had our hands full of kids, but my mind was still set on moving back home, and I couldn't stop thinking about it.

Finally, the perfect management level law enforcement position in my exact field became available to all qualified applicants, and it was only thirty miles outside of 20 Cedar St. It was where I wanted my family and myself to live forever. I put the finishing touches on my resume and submitted all the necessary paperwork. I was truly ready to go home and I couldn't get 20 Cedar St out of my head.

The very next day I received a phone call from the States attorney office. They had called to let me know that Vincent Jr's belonging's, after nearly six years, had finally been released from the evidence locker. I took care of all the necessary paperwork, and in ten days I received the package at my front door. I locked myself in my bedroom and opened it. One cut blue t-shirt, one cut pair of cut plaid shorts, one cut leather belt, and one pair of black Nike sneakers covered in asphalt. All I wanted was something of sentimental value, just maybe a photo, but all I got to remember him by was the cut up clothes he died in. Maybe that was a better piece of sentimental value though, a message from him to me of how "Not to behave". The only property which was salvaged was the clothes he was wearing when his killer launched him off his truck. I held closely onto his belongings as if I was holding my cousin when he was unconscious on the pavement and cried. Shortly after, I decided to package his clothes and kept them in my bedroom closet so he could always be with me and never be left alone again. My cousin and I both wore the same size sneakers, and I believed that I had found a way for us to stay together. I decided to wear his sneakers at times, especially when I needed him by my side.

A few days after receiving my cousin's belongings, I was contacted by an individual who claimed to be my half-brother from my deceased father. He was about six years older than I was and wanted to let me know who he was, so we could have a brotherly relationship after a nearly forty year wait. I told him that I had no desire to meet or speak to my other half siblings from my drug addict father, and had no desire to meet him either. I explained to him that there was no way that I considered him my brother just because my biological father had children with three different women. I let him know how I felt, but he didn't agree. I ended the conversation and that was the way it stayed. He had a few pictures of himself posted on a social media site and I decided to look at them, but not because I cared, just because I never believed I had the same father as my sisters, due to our different genetic features. At that point in my life, I had seen all six of my father's children that I knew of, to include myself. Every single one of his kids had dark hair with dark eyes, were somewhat hairy, and very strongly resembled my father's side of the family, except for me. I had light hair, colored eyes, and couldn't grow even close to a full beard if my life depended on it.

After finally seeing the last piece of the puzzle, the latest half-brother, I decided that I needed to run a DNA test to see if I really was a child of my drug addict father, or if I was the product of a possible one-night stand. I asked my younger sister if she would take a DNA test if I paid for it, and I explained to her that I just wanted to know. She agreed, and I paid for the tests and had them shipped overnight to our separate locations. We both completed the cheek swabs and sent the DNA tests back to the lab the very next day. It didn't matter to me if I was the son of my drug addict father or not, but I wanted to know if there were any more lies or anything else I didn't know about myself. The results were back within a few weeks and I found out that indeed, I was my father's son, ninety-nine point nine percent. I must've just taken all of my grandfather's genetics. My great-grandfather, grandfather, Uncle Vincent, Vincent Jr, and myself, got nearly the same features. I guess that I was more comfortable looking like the men from the side of my family that I was around as a child. The results also let me know that my mother may have been a drug addict, but at least she wasn't sleeping around with random men, and I am able to respect her for that.

A few months after I received the DNA results, my younger sister found an old copy of the obituary of my father. It was the same obituary that I never read, the one that I tossed into the trash many years earlier when stationed overseas in the military. My younger sister had sent me the obituary to point out a certain paragraph mentioning my father's children. I decided to read it nearly seventeen years after his death and noticed that the half-brother who had recently contacted me was actually mentioned in the obituary. He was mentioned as the oldest child of my father. The only thing I received from knowing that information was just once again, that I didn't care. It only proved the fact that I didn't care years ago when I never read the obituary and I still didn't care about my father or his other kids today.

About three months had gone by since I applied for that perfect job near 20 Cedar St and I was awaiting an answer any day. In the meantime, I had seen that my brother Tony had been arrested many times within a few months. I tried locating him but wasn't able to get in touch, the courts had already released him back to the streets. I believed that I would never hear from my brother Tony again, unless it was from the authorities notifying me of his death.

While waiting the final days to hear back from the 20 Cedar St job, I took a long hard look at my kids swimming in our pool that summer afternoon. I noticed how much fun my children were having and realized that they could give two craps about 20 Cedar St. I started to think about my wife and children, and began to understand that they didn't care where they lived, they just wanted to be together and happy. I thought to myself and discovered that a real family is all I ever wanted when I was a kid. I said to my wife the next day, "This is the job I want, and 20 Cedar St is definitely the area in which I want to live, but I finally realized what's truly important." I explained to my wife that our family will end up where we end up. I then said, "It's alright if I don't get the 20 Cedar St job, what matters is that we're all together." I had decided that whatever happened in the next few days, would be the last time I would ever try to force my family to live in the 20 Cedar St area, simply because of my personal emotions.

Chapter 16

I was at work, sitting at my desk when I received the decision in which I wasn't selected for that perfect management position near 20 Cedar St. I stared at the computer screen for a few minutes and thought about a whole lot, then deleted the emailed message. I called my wife at home and told her that the agency decided to select someone else for the job. I told her that she could finally decorate our house the way she had always wanted over the years, because we were home. I then understood that being home meant being together, and pondered over the idea that maybe I wasn't supposed to go back to 20 Cedar St to begin with. It was quite possible that someone or something was keeping me away from the cursed home. Either way, it was the first time in many years that I was able to live for just one day, not worrying about if I would ever get back to 20 Cedar St.

I had taken the last four or five years away from my family, because all I could think about was going home. I had been so out of control about returning to the 20 Cedar St area, that my children were talking about it at school as well. I wouldn't even let my wife hang pictures on the wall, because I refused to call anywhere but 20 Cedar St home. My brain was finally able to relax, and I knew where I belonged, with my family. At the same time though, I had asked myself if those reasons were really good enough for me to stay away from 20 Cedar St. I said to myself, "I could just keep applying for more positions until one finally falls through." My mind still needed to get clearer, because not all of my questions about myself or my past were completely answered yet. If I was really going to call somewhere other than 20 Cedar St home, I needed to close my childhood chapters and move on with my life. I had to come up with my own answers about 20 Cedar St. I went all the way back to the days when I was just a kid, thought about everything I had dealt with, and wanted to know why everything happened the way it did. I wanted to know the history of how the curse of 20 Cedar St came about, which struck down upon the people living inside the home. I wanted to know where the spading fork was, which I still believe put those puncture wounds into my mother's body. I needed to know why I was the only 20 Cedar St man in over one-hundred years to be able to change my criminal-like ways. Why was I given so many chances, and what was I hear to do on this earth? I thought about the priest who didn't fully understand the favor he was doing by creating an additional cremation plot at the cemetery, which was proof to me that my brother would die soon enough. I thought even more about the curse of 20 Cedar St that my grandmother would talk about so often, but I had to come up with my own answers. I had learned a lot on my own over the years, especially from my own mistakes, and didn't learn much at all from being guided or taught decent things.

After years of being a father, I started to understand more about the curse. I began to realize that maybe my 20 Cedar St ancestors broke the law and made each wrong decision knowingly and without guidance, just as I did in my younger days. I also realized that every 20 Cedar St adult had failed to pass down and teach their children from the knowledge they had gained from their own mistakes. That is exactly what went on inside the walls of 20 Cedar St as a child, no talking, no teaching, and no knowing. I began realizing that every 20 Cedar St generation only cared about themselves and never truly cared about the future and well-being of the children that they forced into this world. My great-grandparents, grandparents, and parents must not have thought that their children were worth the headache. My grandparents were the greatest and kindest people in the world to me. They are heroes to me and I miss them every single day. At the same time though, if my grandparents would've cared to correct the problems of their own children instead of hiding them, they wouldn't have had to do anything at all for me. That is one of the reasons I tell my children on a daily basis, "Lazy people work twice as much, because they have to do the job all over again."

As I scanned over the past one-hundred years of

cursed mistakes and criminal behavior which plagued 20 Cedar St, I was finally able to come up with an accurate realization to one of my largest unanswered questions. Was there a curse casted upon everyone inside of 20 Cedar St until the final person moved out? My answer had become very clear to me at that moment, "No, there was never a curse." Some of my ancestors may have believed there was a curse, but I then understand that they didn't want to take responsibility for their own actions and poor parenting. My 20 Cedar St ancestors were never able to talk to their children, give advice, share stories of knowledge, or help each other in any way. They wouldn't believe or see the truth about themselves in the mirror, or about their children who they were supposed to guide throughout eternity. The facts had become very clear. My grandparents wanted to believe that they were great parents and that their children were perfect, but they never thought, cared, or wanted, to truly be part of their children's lives. They thought that hiding their own problems and their children's inside the walls of 20 Cedar St would be the best thing to do.

Each and every ancestor from 20 Cedar St took the long and tiresome canoe ride down shortcut lane. The shortcuts they took in caring for the honest well-being of their children, was another prime example of how every 20 Cedar St generation was set up for failure. Not a single 20 Cedar St child was ever equipped to enter the real world without having to learn from their own costly mistakes. Without simple conversation, we had to learn the unknowingly hard way, and for most of us, it became too late to repair the damage we had already done to ourselves.

I can still remember the only piece of advice that my grandfather ever told my older brother and myself, he said that "Drugs and alcohol were poison." But, I can also remember when my brother and I would come home messed up, and my grandfather wouldn't say anything about it, not a care in the world. I wish someone would've smacked the hell out of me for coming home drunk at the age of thirteen. I wish somebody would've told me what a screw up I was, but nobody ever did.

My grandfather was a great person and again, is a hero to me, but he should have looked back at his own gambling addiction and fixed that first. He should have made the effort to intervene into his drug addicted children's lives, instead of running his gambling enterprise all those years.

My grandfather thought it was necessary to teach me how to bet on race dogs as a young kid, as I would run his bets from the track to the ticket counter. I may have learned some forms of gambling from him, but instead, I wish he would've shown me how to use the one and only screwdriver he had in his closet. Even though my grandparents loved their children and were the greatest and kindest people to me, they were enabling individuals who continued the same bad parenting that was probably taught to them.

Every man who came from 20 Cedar St to include the men who married into my family were either convicted felons, had criminal arrests, or continued illegal activity until they day they died, except for me. I realized that I wasn't destined to get into any trouble for my criminal-like behavior when I was younger. I again thought to myself, "Why am I the first to be able to stop, why did I never get caught, I must be meant for something more, but what?" I do acknowledge that I am no better than the rest of the men from 20 Cedar St, just plain old lucky. I was given the gift of fortune and was allowed to live a life with many chances. I am so proud of myself for changing and it was definitely worth the wait. I have learned much more than the average bear and love the person I have finally become. I can admit that I am not perfect though. I still have a horrible temper at times, but it is being controlled better every day. I have become an extremely paranoid individual, because I have seen the road where I could've continued down, and I never want to end up there. Whenever I make even the simplest decisions; I cross examine every possible outcome to ensure a positive ending. I do admit that I still have plenty of unresolved issues from my childhood. My paranoia causes me to guard the home that my family and I live in as if it was the Vatican. A single unexpected knock on my front door brings me to chaos, and I immediately go into a protective rage. I am moderately obsessive compulsive, and have to do so many things a certain way. I have to do things very particular to ensure that I don't change the outcome of the good fortune I've had. I throw out curse words when I'm upset and am trying so hard to correct my language. I have been able to conquer so many of my issues, but know that I'll have to continue working at it for the remainder of my time.

I can finally accept living far away from the 20 Cedar St home that I thought was responsible for everyone's mistakes and behavior all those years. I have come to realize that it doesn't matter if I live near 20 Cedar St or if I live anywhere else in this world. I now understand what matters, and it's that I am together with the family that I brought into this world. I will teach my children from my lessons learned and the wisdom my story empowered me with. I will put myself between my children's problems and cause all the waves necessary to see their water calm, without a ripple. I understand that my children can and probably will have waves that I cannot fix, but I will teach them how to ride them cautiously and educated.

My 20 Cedar St ancestor's problems were similar to a giant snowball rolling down a mountain, getting larger each rotation it took. I decided not to roll downhill anymore, but to start climbing back to

191

the top.

My parents forced me into this world and cared more about drugs than they did about me. I realize that my children don't owe me a damn thing, they didn't ask to come into this world, but were forced into it. It is now my responsibility to ensure that my children have all the tools necessary to become the young adult I wish I could've been. I'm proud of myself for changing and turning into who I am today, but I do regret having to remember the person I was. I was lucky enough to have caught myself before it was too late. I have come to understand that we only have one life to live and then it just might be over for good. I will enjoy it for myself and do it right for my children and future generations to come. I have no doubt in my mind that I will continue to overcome the past one-hundred years of ridiculous 20 Cedar St behavior.

I hope that the 20 Cedar St area cold case unit will stop chasing after what they believe is an elderly man still on the loose for the murder of my mother. The 20 Cedar St area newspaper has put out articles at times, letting everyone know that my mother's killer has almost been found. What the cold case unit will never tell anyone, because they will never figure it out, is that they are looking for a ghost. If they want to find the real murderer of my mother, they can simply take a drive to the 20 Cedar St local cemetery and dig up my uncle Vincent's cremations. I have no intentions of visiting or living in the 20 Cedar St area any time soon, and finally understand that my family and I will end up wherever is best for us.

I still think about the spading fork that hung on the garage wall of 20 Cedar St. I realized that there was one remaining location at 20 Cedar St that I had never searched when I was trying to locate the truth about my mother's death. I believe that my uncles spading fork just might be in the attic of the garage where it hung for so many years. I believe that the spading fork contains DNA and was at the scene. I also believe that if we had a spaded shovel hanging on our garage wall instead of a spading fork, that my mother's body would've never been found. Digging dirt with a spading fork is no better than eating soup with a kitchen fork.

It's been nearly thirty years since my mother was murdered, and I might be the only living person in this world to believe my uncle Vincent killed his own sister. I understand that the spading fork could be at the bottom of some lake, but believe that it just might be in our family's 20 Cedar St garage attic. Whatever the outcome is, I believe my grandparents knew exactly what happened the day a brother and sister left home to get their methadone fix, and only one returned.

After one-hundred years of 20 Cedar St failure, I was the first and only male to hack into my own brains computer and decipher through all the years of knowledge that was never passed down to future generations. I now understand why I never got into any trouble for my criminal-like behavior. It was so I could write this book and help to end one family's ridiculous behavior at a time. I am going to give my children the opportunity to make their way through life with a clear mind. I was placed on this earth to show anyone capable of understanding, that it is never too late to change for the better. Change is not just for ourselves, it also benefits our loving family members and the people who care about us. I hope that other individuals that grew up in a dysfunctional family can read this book and see that there are so many of us out there. The nasty stories we can all tell about our past should not be the same stories that our children have to tell about their own. Even though I cannot get 20 Cedar St out of my head completely, I have realized that time must and will go on.

I have learned so much on this ride, but still tell myself that if I don't learn at least one new thing each day, then I am not satisfied with myself, and if I don't teach my children the one thing I learned that day, then I've failed as a father. There is one thing that I can definitely and proudly say, I have not broken the law in any way, shape, or form, since the day I found out that my first and oldest son was mine. I don't drink, smoke, use drugs, steal, speed, or behave like my past criminal-like past. I am very proud to say that I have never cheated on my wife and have no intentions on ever doing so. I don't want my children to grow up with the feeling of loneliness like I had inside. That is one of the reasons why I tell my children that I love them and give each a hug and kiss as soon as they wake up, and I do the same every night before they fall asleep. One day when my children are older, I will allow them to read this book, and I hope it will allow them to understand even clearer, why I am the way I am.

I don't want my children to become great when it's too late, my job as their father is to give them the opportunity to become great now. I want nothing but the best for my children and will never stop teaching them until the day that I die. Even though children and adults will make their own decisions, I will have done my job as a parent to have taught my kids the outcome to every possible scenario. I will have equipped them with an arsenal of tools and wisdom to become healthy and successful.

It's quite possible that over the next one-hundred years, future generations after myself won't have to learn from unacceptable behavior or their own costly mistakes, but will learn from the wise stories of truth passed down from their ancestor, Jason Salvino. I have finally come to realize that the last one-hundred years of bad personal decisions that my 20 Cedar St family made was never a curse, but just a simple word that we can all understand, "Life."

The End

ABOUT THE AUTHOR

Hello and thank you for reading my true story. I hope I was able to relate to someone out there who has dealt with a similar life as my 20 Cedar St family and I have. So much of my childhood was hidden from me and now I want others to know the story that took me so long to understand. It was my pleasure telling this story and I respectfully want to let everyone know that it is never too late to change for the better.

When writing this book, I didn't want to take any time away from my kids. I decided to wake up early in the morning about four days per week, and would write for a couple hours at a time, until about two years later when 20 Cedar St was complete. There was absolutely so much more that I could've written about, but just didn't feel the need to say too much. I could only imagine the story that my brother Tony could write, but the big difference between our lives is that he will probably never have a good ending.

My brother Tony continues to have multiple arrests for theft and possession of illegal substances. He is constantly serving prison sentences and doesn't seem to want to change. His drug use, along with a blatant stealing rage over the past decade has been fueled by his addiction to heroin. I am not willing to chase or try to help a person that doesn't want to help himself. I will always be willing to help my brother Tony if he ever decides that he wants change in his life. I don't have enough money to help my brother financially, but I will always be there to help him with emotional support and guidance. He knows where I am and how to get into contact with me. My grandfather's final 20 Cedar St area burial plot will always be waiting for him.

I am no longer the young adult I once was before and love the mindset that I have matured into. I am no longer the scared coward I once was and live a life without fear for myself. I do fear death, but the only part of it that terrifies me, is not being on this earth to watch my kids grow up. I am so proud of myself for everything I have accomplished because I know the other road I could've went down.

I have learned to forgive, but will never forget. I have absolutely no hard feelings towards anyone. I forgive my uncle Vincent for what he did to his son and what I believe he did to my mother. I forgive my mother and father for choosing drugs over me. Last but not least, I hope that I can be forgiven as well.

I might not be rich in the bank, but I hit the jackpot with a great wife and incredible children. I know who I am today, and there will be nothing but good memories from here on out, and those I will keep to myself.

58305434R00120

Made in the USA
Charleston, SC
06 July 2016